This book is about your journey
to become a young Jewish woman
who is strong in mind, body, and spirit.

This book was read by

_____
(YOUR NAME)

when

_____
(OCCASION)

This book was a loving gift from

_____

THE JGirl's Guide

The Young Jewish Woman's Handbook for Coming of Age

Penina Adelman,
Ali Feldman and
Shulamit Reinharz

JEWISH LIGHTS Publishing
Woodstock, Vermont

The JGirl's Guide:
The Young Jewish Woman's Handbook for Coming of Age

2006 Third Printing
2006 Second Printing
2005 First Printing
© 2005 by Brandeis University

Grateful acknowledgment is given for permission to reprint from the following sources: Kadya Molodowsky, from "Women-Poems" and "The Sabbath Song" in *Paper Bridges*, ed. and trans. Kathryn Hellerstein (Detroit: Wayne State University Press, 1999), pages 79, 81, 453, and 455. Dvora Weisberg, "The Study of Torah as a Religious Act" and Itka Frajman Zygmuntowicz, "Survival and Memory," in *Four Centuries of Jewish Women's Spirituality,* ed. Ellen Umansky and Dianne Ashton (Boston: Beacon Press, 1992), pages 276–278 and 222. © 1992 by Ellen M. Umansky and Dianne Ashton. Reprinted by permission from *A Spiritual Life* by Merle Feld, the State University of New York Press. © 1999 the State University of New York Press. All rights reserved. The Chicago Historical Society, for permission to reprint materials from the Emily Frankenstein papers [manuscript], 1915–1920. Rachel Shnider, for material from "Celebrating Our Cycles: A Jewish Woman's Introduction to Menstruation and Womanhood," unpublished manuscript; and Rachel Shnider, "How I Feel about Sex and Sexuality." © 2002 by Rachel Shnider. "Letter to the Front," reprinted by permission of International Creative Management, Inc. © 1978 by Muriel Rukeyser.

Library of Congress Cataloging-in-Publication Data
Adelman, Penina V. (Penina Villenchik)
The Jgirl's guide : the young Jewish woman's handbook for coming of age / Penina Adelman, Ali Feldman, and Shulamit Reinharz.
p. cm.
Includes bibliographical references.
ISBN 1-58023-215-9 (pbk.)
1. Jewish girls—Conduct of life—Juvenile literature. 2. Jewish girls—Religious life—Juvenile literature. 3. Coming of age—Juvenile literature. I. Feldman, Ali. II. Reinharz, Shulamit. III. Title.
BM727.A33 2005
296.7'0835'2—dc22   2005001674

Manufactured in the United States of America
Cover design: Asya Blue

Published by Jewish Lights Publishing
A Division of LongHill Partners, Inc.
Sunset Farm Offices, Route 4, P.O. Box 237
Woodstock, VT 05091
Tel (802) 457-4000   Fax (802) 457-4004
www.jewishlights.com

CONTENTS

8▶

THINKING BEFORE I SPEAK: I need to say what
I feel and think, but I may be hurting
people when I do.   120

Mitzvah: *Shmirat halashon* (guarding the tongue)

Guarding Your Tongue • *Lashon Hara* • How to Combat *Lashon
Hara* • The Consequences of Gossip • Silence

9▶

GETTING INVOLVED: I want to make the world
a better place, but there are just too
many problems.   134

Mitzvot: *Tikkun olam* (repairing the world);
Kol Israel areivim zeh lazeh (all of Israel are responsible for
one another)

Make a Difference • Putting the World Back Together •
Volunteering • Jewish Women Who Are Changing the World

10▶

BECOMING MYSELF: I am Jewish, but is this
how I want to identify myself?   149

Mitzvot: Bat mitzvah (becoming a Jewish
woman); *Talmud Torah* (Torah study)

Identifying Yourself • What Makes You Happy to Be a Jew? •
Bat Mitzvah • Women and Torah Study • Studying Torah

PREFACE

I am a professor, a daughter, a mother, a sister, a wife, an aunt, a friend, and many other things. I'm also a JGirl—and probably you are, too. You can be a JGirl as soon as you're born and stay at it your whole life. You can become a JGirl later. Everybody's story is different.

Being a JGirl means thinking about the fact that you are Jewish and wanting to find out more about other Jews. It means getting excited when you discover that a competitor at the Olympics is a young Jewish person and wondering how she lives her life. It means wanting to look up the Jewish community if you travel to another country. It means reading the newspaper with a special eye for what is going on in Israel or Jewish communities in other countries.

The JGirl's Guide is for girls who have always been JGirls and for those who want to become JGirls. It's for learning what it takes to become one. It's written with you in mind.

I started on my JGirl path from the minute I was born in a Catholic hospital in Amsterdam, Holland. Both my parents had escaped from Germany as teenagers when the Nazis gained power. They thought they would be safe in Holland, but after they arrived there, the Nazis invaded that country as well. My parents (who were actually only boyfriend and girlfriend at the time) decided to hide rather than give up, just like Anne Frank did with her family. Unlike Anne Frank, however, the people who would become my parents were never caught. Thus, when the war was finally over and the Jews could come out of their hiding places, my parents married, and nine months later I was born. With a history like that and with my parents giving me a Hebrew name—Shulamit—I was off and running as a JGirl.

Later, when we moved to the United States, I started going to public school during the day and Hebrew school on two afternoons and Sunday mornings. Unlike some kids, I loved it. It was great to learn a new language and be able to be a leader in Junior Congregation. Each time we participated in Junior Congregation, a star was put on a chart. I was pretty ambitious and loved getting those stars.

Then one day I turned 12 and it was time to start preparing for my bat mitzvah. Life was very different then from the way it is now. I sat with a teacher who gave me a phonograph recording (not even a tape and certainly not a CD) to learn my Haftarah. That was pretty much my entire training. Girls didn't do as much for their bat mitzvah ceremonies in the 1950s, when I had mine, as they do now. In those days, many girls didn't even become bat mitzvah at all.

During the summer in which I turned 12, my mother, baby brother, and I traveled to Israel to visit relatives and see the country. By ship it took two weeks to get there and two weeks to get back—with lots of seasickness along the way. I returned from Israel a very enthusiastic JGirl. Israel was 10 years old, and I was 12. I had lots of adventures in the *moshav* (rural town) I visited, including riding horses, building and sitting around campfires, and hanging out with Israeli kids. I loved everything Israeli. So when the movie *Exodus* came out, I went to see it and, of course, fell in love with that, too. I decided then and there that I would try to marry someone who shared the same ideas I did.

When I was 15 and living in a New Jersey suburb, I met an Israeli boy who had just moved to the United States. We became friends right away because he hadn't learned English yet, and I had learned enough Hebrew in Hebrew school and from my trip to Israel that we could communicate. After we graduated from college, we married, and later we had two daughters. We gave them Hebrew names (Yael and Naomi). They too became JGirls.

As a professor at Brandeis University in Waltham, Massachusetts, I teach sociology and women's studies. Many of the topics I study relate to issues that were important to me growing up. In 1997, I created a special research center to examine issues central to Jews and to women (the Hadassah-Brandeis Institute). Each summer we invite a few highly talented college students to work with us as interns. That's how this book, *The JGirl's Guide,* was born.

One of the interns was Ali Feldman, a young woman from Toronto, who came to work with us on new ideas she was developing for bat mitzvah girls. By the end of the summer, Ali had finished the first draft of a huge book on the topic. The next summer, she returned to continue her work, and I recommended that she contact Penina Adelman, a local professional who had a bat mitzvah–age daughter of her own and had run groups for mothers and daughters. Since then Penina and Ali have worked hard to turn that first draft into a book of manageable size that girls can use wherever they live. I have tried to be helpful throughout the whole process.

Why did I ask Penina and Ali to spend so much time writing this book for you? The reasons are simple.

No matter how much has been written about being a Jewish girl, there is always need for more, because the lives of Jewish teens are constantly changing. When I was growing up there were no cell phones, videos, DVDs, digital cameras, Internet, computers, fax machines, or instant messaging. Most families had only one car; most moms didn't work outside the home. Hebrew day schools were very rare. Fewer JGirls grew up in divorced families, with single moms or stepparents. More JGirls now than earlier grow up in families with two moms or two dads. Because life is changing so quickly, it is important to think about what it means to be a JGirl today.

A second reason that I urged Ali and Penina to work on this book is that some Jewish girls grow up in places where there aren't many Jewish kids. That was true for me. I didn't have many other Jewish girls to talk to, so I could have used this book. However, no one wrote it for me, so I decided to work with Ali and Penina on writing this for you.

We'd love to hear from you. Tell us your JGirl story. Perhaps we can pass it on to other girls as we work on building a fabulous JGirl world!

SHULAMIT REINHARZ

ACKNOWLEDGMENTS

This book began as Ali Feldman's project when she was an intern at the Hadassah-Brandeis Institute. I am grateful to Ali for asking me to work with her and for being a wonderful co-author and *hevruta*. I am grateful to Diane Troderman, Harold Grinspoon, and the Grinspoon Foundation for providing the funds to enable me to work on this book for two years. During two summers, I engaged the efforts of Lily Safra Interns at the Hadassah-Brandeis Institute: Naomi Reinharz at Brown University, Aviva Dautch at Leo Baeck College, and Rosie Davis at Bates College. Two Student-Scholar Partners at Brandeis University also helped a great deal: Miriam Kingsberg and Amy Schiller.

Nancy Vineberg was instrumental in negotiating all the publishing details with Jewish Lights and particularly with Stuart M. Matlins, publisher, and his very talented staff, especially Emily Wichland and Amanda Dupuis, who oversaw this project.

Rabbi Benjamin Samuels helped find sources on the *mitzvot* and clarified many Jewish concepts for me. Rabbi Karen Landy advised me on writing for girls on sexual issues. Abby Wyschogrod, Nechama Cheses, and Vicky Lyon were simultaneously going through the bat mitzvah process with their daughters and shared their insights with me. Stephanie Samuels and Elkie Zarchi shared their experience in teaching Jewish girls. Melissa Klapper was very generous in contributing her knowledge of Jewish-American girls' diaries to the book. Many girls read and critiqued the manuscript: Gabrielle Goodman of Manhattan as well as the Focus Group Girls at Temple Shalom in Milton, Massachusetts, and at the Rashi School in Newton, Massachusetts.

The Women's Studies Research Center at Brandeis University and the Hadassah-Brandeis Institute provided me with space, time and supportive, stimulating colleagues who constantly remind me what the work is for. I presented *The JGirl's Guide* to them at various stages and they were wonderful, discerning critics. Shula Reinharz—my co-author, as well as the director of both the Women's Studies Research Center at Brandeis University and the Hadassah-Brandeis Institute—kept the goals of this book in front of us always.

My mother, Selma Williams, continues to be my mentor.

Last, but not least, Steve Adelman, my patron and critic was there by my side.

This book is dedicated to Laura, my precious guide.

Penina Adelman

The everlasting wisdom of *Pirkei Avot* assists me in expressing my gratitude to the many people involved in *The JGirl's Guide*.

Aseh l'cha rav—Appoint a teacher for yourself (*Pirkei Avot* 1:6). Several people have mentored and guided me through this project. Dr. Shulamit Reinharz was the motivating force. She met me as an amateur writer and saw great potential in this project. It is due to her vision that the book is before you today. Her constant effort to ensure funding, her insightful comments, and her dream of paving the way for a healthy and happy future for girls have seen this project through to fruition. Many other people in Boston, Toronto, Montreal, and Jerusalem acted as mentors and advisers: Dr. Susan Kahn, Dr. Sylvia Barack Fishman, Helene Greenberg, Sylvia Fuchs Fried, Greg Beiles, Dr. Nora Gold, Rabbi Tziv Hirshfield,

Dr. David Bernstein, Dr. Barry Chazan, Dr. Susan Wall, Gila Silverman, Nancy Vineberg, Barbara Berley Melitz, Diane Troderman and people at the Toronto Heschel School, Pardes Institute for Jewish Studies, Nishmat Midrasha for women's studies, and the Hadassah-Brandeis Institute.

V'hetalech min ha safek—And remove yourself from uncertainty (*Pirkei Avot* 1:16). I would like to mention three rabbis who have been personally and professionally helpful to me: Rabbi Reuven Tradburks of Kehillat Shaarei Torah in Toronto, Rabbi Yehoshua Berman, and Rabbi Tzvi Leshem.

Koneh l'cha chaver—Acquire a friend for yourself (*Pirkei Avot* 1:6). Several friends and colleagues reviewed this work, challenged my ideas, and provoked me to think about girls, Judaism, and *mitzvot* in a vibrant light. In particular, I would like to thank my Jerusalem friends, with whom I was privileged to share an intellectual, spiritual, musical, and rational journey to Judaism for the three years I lived there.

I am grateful to the AviChai Foundation for sponsoring the Pardes Educators Program, and other foundations that made this project possible—in particular, the Harold Grinspoon Foundation and the Edmond J. Safra Foundation, as well as Lily Safra and Jeff Keil.

Stuart M. Matlins, publisher; Emily Wichland; Shelly Angers; Amanda Dupuis; and the team at Jewish Lights Publishing produced this project with finesse and excellence. Their meticulous and creative editing skills made *The JGirl's Guide* come to life! I am grateful for their commitment and effort and feedback given to our book.

It is rare that two authors have the same vision and same passion and can see eye-to-eye through to the publication of a book, yet Penina and I were blessed to have such an experience. Penina is a genuine *chevruta* partner: one who is able to challenge me, point out areas of improvement, and grow with me at the same time. Although we both experienced labor pains, long nights, writer's block, and some frustrations, Penina was a perfect partner to share this journey with.

And thanks to all the JGirls who responded to e-mails, reviewed sample chapters, brought me up to date on the latest lingo, and kept me inspired to create this work: Laura Adelman, Naomi Reinharz, Emily Wise, Amanda Wise, Lisa Herberman, Stacey Herberman, Perry Sasson, Ariela Lovett, Emily Larson, Tamar Gaffin-Cahn, Sarah Perez, Eytal Timberg, Matan Daniel, and Adina Roussos.

This book is dedicated to my family who ground me and lift me up at the same time, who have embraced our rich Jewish heritage with me, and whose friendship, wisdom, and parenting I feel are my greatest blessings. Each day they inspire me with their own love of Judaism, life, and the world. Thank you to my parents, Ann and Joe Feldman, my siblings, Jess, Avner, Sarah, and Benji, and to my grandparents, Helen and Joe Morgan. May they be blessed with many years of good health and fulfillment.

We are a fortunate generation: one that is free to express, embrace, and explore our Judaism. We have a wealth of resources and opportunities, from which I personally have benefited greatly. It is my greatest prayer that the book serves its purpose: to open our minds to how fun, exciting, and special it is to be a Jewish girl today.

ALI FELDMAN

I have always been intrigued by Jewish Lights because of the relevance of their books to understanding and promoting Jewish life. I am deeply grateful to Stuart M. Matlins, publisher, who immediately grasped the potential of *The JGirl's Guide* and became a wonderful colleague over the course of its completion. Stuart not only brought our book into the Jewish Lights family, he also brought talented editors and expert readers on board: Emily Wichland, Lauren Seidman, Amanda Dupuis, Bryna Fischer, Sally Friedman, and Judith Antonelli. *The JGirl's Guide* would not be the excellent book I think it is without their hard work and skilled input.

No project of this nature could move forward without financial assistance, and for this I have to thank Diane Troderman, the founding chair of the board of the Hadassah-Brandeis Institute, and the Harold Grinspoon Foundation, for their early and generous support.

Penina Adelman has been resident scholar at the Brandeis University Women's Studies Research Center for many years. In that time she has brought to bear her experience as a leader of mother-daughter Bat Mitzvah groups and as the author of *Miriam's Well: Rituals for Jewish Women around the Year* and a forthcoming book on *Eishet Chayil*. It has been my pleasure to work with Penina on many projects throughout the years and I look forward to many more.

I have watched Ali Feldman blossom from an enthusiastic undergraduate student to a dedicated teacher. This book started as Ali's intern project at the Hadassah-Brandeis Institute and I feel privileged to have shared this dream and journey with her.

I am extremely fortunate that Nancy Vineberg signed on to be the Hadassah-Brandeis Institute's Director of Communications and Strategic Development a few years ago. Her actual role transcends her title: she's the HBI's right-hand, transforming rough ideas into polished reality. Thank you, Nancy, for your stewardship of this project.

Finally, I would like to dedicate my work on this book to my mother, Ilse Rothschild, who taught me to be a Jewish girl, and to my two daughters, Yael and Naomi, whom I have tried to teach myself. May they be blessed with daughters of their own one day.

SHULAMIT REINHARZ

INTRODUCTION

I'm a Jewish girl and so I'll become a Jewish woman—is there any more to it than that?

WELCOME

Dear JGirl,

Welcome to The JGirl's Guide, *a book for you to read and experiment with, written in part by girls your age.*

The idea for this book began one summer when I was an intern at the Hadassah-Brandeis Institute. I wanted Jewish girls to have something I had not had: a life-changing Jewish coming-of-age experience.

My bat mitzvah was fun. There were tons of gifts, great food, and a lot of dancing. I don't remember anything particularly Jewish about it; it could have been a giant birthday party. However, it did start me

thinking about being Jewish. I began to wonder, "Where do I fit in?"
I was a Conservative Jew. Being Conservative was just what my par-
ents and grandparents did, so I had my bat mitzvah in the
Conservative synagogue to which we belonged. In the summers I
attended a Zionist camp. My grandparents were Holocaust survivors,
so I became interested in finding out more about my roots and heritage.

After my bat mitzvah, I had the feeling that I had missed an
important opportunity to pause before I went from being a Jewish girl
to a young Jewish woman. Something was missing, but I didn't know
what. I never spoke about it. My parents would have been disap-
pointed; my teachers would not have understood; my friends would
not have been interested. At least, that's how I felt.

As I became a teenager, I searched endlessly for some valuable
advice or wisdom. I went outside Judaism to other sources in order to
find something relevant to my life as a young Jewish girl. During
high school, so many situations arose in which I could have used
some decent advice. I didn't realize how many challenging situations
I would confront. In the first week of high school I was offered my first
cigarette, a kiss from a boy, and pressure to join one group of friends
over another. It would have been great to have a book, a person, or a
resource to turn to that spoke my language and tackled head on the
issues I was facing.

After graduating from high school I traveled to Israel to learn
more. Living in Jerusalem was a very rich experience. I loved being
there on Shabbat and feeling the special silence and beauty of the day.
Jewish tradition was everywhere. I decided to go into Jewish education
and become a day-school teacher because I love kids. Working toward
that goal, I came to the Hadassah-Brandeis Institute for a summer
and met Penina Adelman, a writer, mother, and social worker. Now
she'll tell you about her link to The JGirl's Guide.

Ali Feldman

Dear JGirl,

When Ali showed me her manuscript, I was very excited because I was in the midst of my daughter Laura's bat mitzvah year. Some of her friends and my friends decided to start a group for girls and moms that would meet each month. The girls were all going to become b-not mitzvah *(plural of bat mitzvah) within the next two years.*

We celebrated holidays together, studied Torah, and learned about famous Jewish women. The girls made a quilt to use as a Torah cover for each girl's bat mitzvah. When I read Ali's guide for Jewish girls, I wanted to be part of what she called the Bat Mitzvah Project right away.

I grew up in the 1960s in a suburb of Boston, Massachusetts, in a family of Jewish atheists, Jews who did not believe in God. My parents' parents came from an Eastern European background. No one taught me anything about being Jewish. When I was in fifth grade and many of my friends were becoming bar and bat mitzvah, I felt left out, and so I insisted that my parents send me to the Reform Hebrew School that my friends attended.

After college I went to Israel for the first time. Before going there, I had never even seen a Shabbat candle lit at home. I decided to learn more about Jewish tradition, and as I got older I became more ritually observant. Now I am part of a Modern Orthodox community in Newton, Massachusetts, where I live with my husband and three children.

I did not have a bat mitzvah ceremony. They were still pretty rare in the 1960s. Partly because my family hardly observed any rituals—no Shabbat, no Passover seder after my grandparents died, and no bat mitzvah for me—I wrote a book for Jewish women called Miriam's Well: Rituals for Jewish Women Around the Year. *It acquainted women and girls with the* Rosh Chodesh *(New Moon) ritual, a monthly celebration dating from biblical times that is especially significant for women.*

When Ali and I met, we realized that we had a lot in common even though we were from different generations. We both wanted to write a book for Jewish girls coming of age, so we decided to become writing partners. The next step was to find someone who believed in us. That was Shulamit Reinharz, director of the Women's Studies Research Center at Brandeis University in Waltham, Massachusetts, and of the Hadassah-Brandeis Institute, where Ali had been an intern. Shulamit helped us to get the support we needed to write the book, and she has been our mentor ever since.

Ali and I wrote this book during a time of extreme violence and worldwide terrorism: bombs in Jerusalem, the 9/11 attack in the United States, and the anthrax panic. We were grateful to be working on The JGirl's Guide. The act of writing it has been and continues to be an affirmation for us that Jewish girls will be turning into Jewish women for a long time to come and that we hope our words can help in that process. The world needs Jewish young women who are self-confident, rooted in humanitarian values, and in search of the places where they can put their talents to the best use.

We have had input from many girls, a group we call our Teen Tzevet (consultant team). Now some of them will tell you their stories.

Shalom,

Penina Adelman

Dear JGirl,

I'm one of the girls from the Teen Tzevet. I've been giving feedback on this book for quite a while. I'm 13, and I live in Livingston, New Jersey. I like reading, singing, music, writing, animals, helping others, and being with my family. Working on The JGirl's Guide was great because my opinion counted for something. I love writing, so I enjoyed putting my thoughts down on paper. (Actually, I put them *down on the computer screen.) Growing up is a tough time for all girls. I think a book like this can make the teenage years less stressful.*

Yours,

Ariela

Dear JGirl,

Hi, I'm Emily or Leah Malka, whichever you prefer. I'm 11, and I live in Holliston, Massachusetts. I love reading and writing long stories, making scrapbooks, and drawing. I also play the piano. I'm interested in large families, multiple births, and the McCaughey septuplets (seven babies born at once). I know, that's a strange interest!

I enjoyed writing for The JGirl's Guide *because as I answered the questions that were posed I was able to think about what I believe about certain subjects. In my opinion, only girls can truly relate to and understand what other girls are thinking and experiencing. It was awesome to be able to share my thoughts on topics relevant to our lives as teenage girls!*

Happy reading!

Emily

Dear JGirl,

I'm 21 and a senior in college studying American civilization and Hispanic studies. My hobbies include learning new things and exploring new cultures, traveling, hanging out and going out with friends, watching movies, listening to music and going to concerts, dancing for fun, and taking part in Jewish and Hispanic culture.

I loved being part of this book. It was really fun to be able to revisit my adolescence and all the issues and concerns I had to deal with at that time. Through books and diaries and pictures, I was able to look back at my own coming of age—at the person I was then and the person I am now—and use that knowledge to try to help Jewish girls who are going through the same thing across the country. I know something like it would have been very helpful to me. Have fun and good luck—in adolescence and beyond!

Yours truly,

Naomi

A Royal Daughter, a JGirl

Who are you? It is rare that we set aside time in our lives to think about who we really are, what makes us unique, and what we want in life. We are all a combination of many forces and influences, such as our families, the media, the music we like, and the activities we do in our free time.

Finding out who we are at our core is a tough task. One formula that Judaism offers to discover who we are is a favorite of ours. It's not some elaborate math equation or physics formula that requires intense analytical thinking. It is a phrase from Psalms: *Kol k'vodah bat melekh p'nimah,* which can be translated as "The true majesty of a royal daughter is inside her" (Psalms 45:14). In modern terms, this means that to feel great about yourself—to feel majestic, even—you need to listen to your inner self.

In some Jewish sources Jewish women are considered to be "daughters of a king," the king being God. Some people are uncomfortable equating God with a king because a king is an authoritarian male figure. However, this is only one way of describing God. God is also described as Warrior, Father, Compassionate One—even Nursing Mother. When we think of God as royalty, that is just one aspect of God. Seeing ourselves as "royal daughters" may help us to explore what feeling like royalty means.

When we discover our inner selves and let our inner voices direct our lives, we become majestic and magnificent. Becoming "a royal daughter" doesn't mean being adorned with jewels and lavish clothing. It means loving who we are inside, appreciating our unique characteristics, and allowing our internal voice to guide our lives. This theme of *Kol k'vodah bat melekh p'nimah* will appear throughout *The JGirl's Guide.*

There are many different definitions of a Jew. Some people define Jews as people who believe in the Jewish religion—but many Jews who do not believe in God still live a Jewish life. What is a Jewish life? Jews come from many different cultures, so their customs differ widely. According to Orthodox and Conservative Judaism, you are Jewish if you have a Jewish mother. According to Reform and Reconstructionist Judaism, you are also Jewish if you have only a Jewish father but are raised as a Jew. A Jew can also be a person who converts to Judaism, like Ruth in the Bible, whom you'll read about in the chapter on friendship. Some people call converts "Jews by choice," but according to Jewish tradition they are Jews, the same as those who are born Jewish, and not to be treated any differently. It has even been noted that in American culture, where assimilation is often so easy and enticing, we are all Jews "by choice"!

One of the fundamental texts of Judaism is the Talmud, and one of the most striking aspects of the Talmud is that when a legal issue is being debated, all opinions about the topic are included, even those that disagree with the majority opinion. *The JGirl's Guide* is like the Talmud in this respect. We present many opinions, viewpoints, and ways of living a Jewish life so that you can learn about the mosaic that is Judaism and make up your own mind about how to be a Jew. This book will not try to change you into a very religious person, nor will it try to take you away from religion. It will not attempt to make you believe in something specific. Instead, we hope that *The JGirl's Guide* will help you to think about what being Jewish means to you. We believe that Judaism can help you to deal with many issues you face today.

Coming of Age

Throughout the world and throughout time, girls have participated in rituals marking their coming of age. A bat mitzvah belongs to this type of ritual. It marks the passage from child to adult, from girl to woman, within the family and community. It is a beginning, not an end. In some coming-of-age rituals, such as the Navaho *Kinaalda,* a girl is believed to become the goddess of fertility and life. Her tribe treats her afterwards as one who holds the power of bringing life into the world.

The Upanayana, or Sacred Thread Ceremony, of the Hindu people in India has been revived in the last 25 years for girls. Now girls as well as boys learn the sacred teachings of their culture and receive a three-stranded thread symbolizing their coming of age. In addition, many communities in Nigeria practice the Fattening Ceremony, in which unmarried girls prepare for womanhood by eating starchy foods and sleeping a lot. This way they embody the ideal woman, who is fat, symbolizing health, wealth, and beauty.

As a bat mitzvah girl, you do not become a goddess. However, you do become filled with the power of Jewish tradition. You embody all the wisdom of the Jewish people up until now. You can demonstrate this by reading Torah, leading prayers, giving a speech about your Torah portion, or doing good deeds on behalf of others. By taking on the responsibility of doing *mitzvot* (the plural of mitzvah)—or more *mitzvot* than you did before—you begin to take your place as a responsible Jewish adult and contribute to your community.

WHAT'S A MITZVAH?

Jewish tradition teaches that before the world was created, there was chaos and confusion. When God created the world, the goal was to establish order and harmony. The world could run properly only when there were guidelines and strategies to structure it and keep it peaceful; that's why the concept of mitzvah was born, according to tradition.

Literally, the word *mitzvah* means a "commandment" given by God. Some people believe that the *mitzvot* are merely imposed rules and laws that may feel restrictive and prevent people from living freely, but the *mitzvot* can actually help us to interact meaningfully and successfully with others, the world around us, and ourselves. They offer excellent advice on how to deal with every situation. They refine our sensitivities. They even can relate to walking the dog, helping with dinner, cleaning your room, and taking out the garbage. They also include taking care of your body, being a great friend, and helping your sibling (if you have one) with homework. Believe it or not, the *mitzvot* can apply to practically all areas of your life. They are guiding principles steeped in ancient wisdom that is still relevant to a modern human.

Each chapter in this book is linked to a mitzvah or several *mitzvot*. The Talmud tells us that there are 613 mitzvot: 248 positive ones—such as "Love your neighbor as yourself" (Leviticus 19:18)—and 365 negative ones—such as "Don't embarrass people" (Leviticus 19:17). Maimonides, who lived in the 12th century and is known as one of the greatest philosophers in Jewish history, listed these 613 mitzvot in his master work, *Sefer Hamitzvot* (The Book of *Mitzvot*), linking each one with its supporting reference in the Bible. The *mitzvot* you will find in this book come from Maimonides's list.

Some of the *mitzvot* deal with ethical issues that are obviously important, such as taking care of orphans and widows. Some refer to details of behavior that might not seem important, like separating a piece of dough from a *challah* (special Shabbat bread) before baking it. Not all of the traditional *mitzvot* are possible to do today, even by the most observant person. Some of them are irrelevant, because they had to do with the Temple in Jerusalem that was destroyed 2,000 years ago. Other *mitzvot* can be done only if you live in Israel.

The word mitzvah is also used more generally to mean "a good thing to do"—as in "It would be a real mitzvah to go over to the new girl sitting alone in the cafeteria and have lunch with her." This kind of mitzvah is specified in the Torah as an act of lovingkindness, treating a stranger well, loving your neighbor as yourself.

The *JGirl's Guide* is a chance for you to see what practical advice and guidance Judaism has to offer as you journey through your adolescent years in our pop-culture world. Just as your body changes during your teen years, so does your personality and soul. In Judaism ages 12 and 13 are perceived as the beginning of maturity; that is why this is the traditional age of bat and bar mitzvah, respectively. Secular society also defines ages of maturity, when you are given the right to drive a car, to vote, to serve in the armed forces, and to drink alcohol.

Just as you can choose to get a driver's license or vote, you can choose to do *mitzvot*. Some Jews choose to follow the *mitzvot* because of their ethical nature, whereas other Jews choose to follow *mitzvot* because they feel good about the structure and discipline it gives to their lives. As a bat mitzvah, at whatever age, you can take on as many or as few *mitzvot* as you like. You are probably carrying out some of them already, simply in the way you live, but carrying out a mitzvah is even more rewarding if you know that you are doing it and why. The point of this book is to give you the information you need so you can make your own decisions about how you choose to be a Jew.

Whether you are about to become a bat mitzvah or have already done so; whether you do it formally in a synagogue with your family and community or quietly through your own Jewish study, *The JGirl's Guide* can give you a fresh perspective and lead you to consider ideas way beyond the notion that being a young Jewish woman today is cool, fun, meaningful, and personal. This book helps you to explore some of the relevant topics in your life and discover Jewish wisdom and guidance on these topics. Did you ever think that there might be Jewish sources or advice on how to deal with your first kiss? Pressure from your friends? Arguing with your parents? This book gives you an opportunity to see your Judaism, adolescence, and femininity combined, in order to become a Jewish woman in the most meaningful way possible.

A FEW HISTORICAL BASICS

If you've had a strong Jewish education, you probably already know the following facts about our history and traditions. If you haven't, this section will give you some background that will provide context for the rest of the chapters in this book.

Our religion originated approximately 4,000 years ago. It began with a few essential people, the patriarchs and matriarchs we learn about in the Bible: Abraham, Sarah, Isaac, Rebecca, Jacob, Leah, and Rachel.

In biblical times we grew, multiplied, and became a nation of tribes. There were righteous characters and sinful ones, role models and villains. After a period of being enslaved in *Mitzrayim* (Egypt), we wandered through the Sinai desert for 40 years and then settled in a Promised Land "flowing with milk and honey," the Land of Israel. In about 900 B.C.E. the First Temple was built in Jerusalem; it was the most prestigious and glamorous center for Jewish life. It was destroyed in 586 B.C.E., and the people were dispersed in the Babylonian Exile. Seventy years later many of the exiles returned, and the Temple was rebuilt. The Second Temple stood for 600 years, until it was destroyed by the Romans in 70 C.E.

After that destruction, our religion adapted to life without a central place of worship. This was the beginning of the rabbinic age. We established great councils of sages who studied the Bible and created books of interpretations and explanations of the Torah. Some of the famous sages of this period were Rabbi Akiva, Rabbi Yochanan ben Zakkai, and Rabbi Yehudah haNasi. Amid the centers of study for men, there were also women who excelled in Torah learning and became an authoritative voice in their communities. Women such as Bruriah, Ima Shalom, Yalta, and Rava's wife (Rabbi Chisola's unnamed daughter) were experts in Jewish law.

The rabbinic age was a rich era filled with scholarship and study. Over several centuries, rabbis and great scholars composed two important works, the Mishnah and the Gemara. Together these form the Talmud and explain the Torah in a much more detailed way. These books were filled with pages of discussion and debate, including many disagreements and alternative opinions. The sages also developed creative explanations that filled in the gaps in Torah stories. This kind of creative explanation is known as midrash.

Later scholars continued the process of commentary and explanation, and the rules they established are the basis of traditional Judaism today. Some of the most famous sages were Rashi (1040–1105), Maimonides (1135–1204), Nachmanides (1195–1270), and Rabbi Yosef Karo (1488–1575).

When the Second Temple was destroyed, the Jews were scattered throughout the world. Gradually they adopted some of the ways of the people and cultures surrounding them. Jews in Spain began speaking Spanish and formed their own Jewish-Spanish language called Ladino. They also began to integrate Spanish customs into their own practices. Jews in Germany began speaking a form of German that became known as Yiddish. Jews in Italy spoke Judeo-Italian and adopted some of the customs of that land. Jews whose customs developed from Spain and other Mediterranean countries became known as Sefardi, and Jews whose practices come from Germany, Russia, and eastern Europe became known as Ashkenazi. Jews from Asia, Persia (Iran), and the Arab countries are sometimes called Mizrachi, or oriental Jews. Ethiopian Jews, cut off from rabbinic Judaism, developed their own practices.

The study of Torah has been a Jewish passion throughout our history. It is one that continues today as rabbis, teachers, and students engage in being "detectives" of Torah. Today Torah learning is much more accessible and available to Jews throughout the world because of the printing press and the Internet.

Over the centuries Jewish life has been filled with joys and sorrows. Sometimes Jewish communities grew and flourished; sometimes they experienced persecution, death, and destruction. The Jewish Enlightenment, an intellectual movement that swept across Europe in the 19th century as Jews were finally permitted to become citizens of some of the countries in which they lived, challenged traditionalists to adopt a more secular, liberal, and open-minded way of life. As a result, the Reform movement was born in Germany, seeking ways for people to maintain a Jewish identity while assimilating to secular Christian cultures. In the United States this movement developed in two different directions: One is the contemporary Reform movement, and the other is the Conservative movement, which evolved as a backlash against Reform's most extreme assimilationist changes. The Reconstructionist movement, which broke off from Conservative Judaism to emphasize Jewishness as a culture, developed in the mid-20th century. While some movements adopted the more liberal ideas of the Western world, another movement evolved that tried to uphold strict adherence to Jewish law while being actively involved in the modern world. Modern Orthodoxy emphasized an unyielding commitment to the strictness of Jewish law, such as how one dresses, prays, and eats, but also encouraged an involvement in the secular studies, professions, and cultures.

Jewish history can be seen as a roller coaster, filled with highs and lows. There are loops of progress, through scholarship, spirituality, and practice, and there are loops of destruction, filled with anti-Semitism, expulsion, and wandering. The roller coaster continues! So now you have a brief overview of Jewish history.

HOW THIS BOOK WORKS

How do you go from being a girl to being a young woman with so many choices and challenges before you? You have more ways to know what's happening in the world, to contact people around the world, and to make your presence felt in the world than any other generation before you. You have more career paths open to you than your grandmother did. Could she have become an astronaut, a surgeon, a rabbi, or a construction worker? You are more accepting than previous generations of alternative lifestyles, homosexuality, single parenthood, adoption, divorce, and other things that used to make people feel ashamed. You have more choices about motherhood, from not having children at all to being a stay-at-home mom, and everything in between. How do you know which decision to make?

Add the Jewish factor and your life just became even more complicated. What does it mean to be Jewish today, let alone to be a Jewish woman?

Your body will take care of your physically becoming a woman, but your physical self still needs help from your mind, heart, and spirit. Where are the models for how to be a Jewish woman today? The public bat mitzvah ceremony is not even a century old—not a very long time in the span of 4,000 years of Jewish history. How did Jewish girls become women in the days of the Bible? How did they become women in the 19th century? How will *you* become a Jewish woman?

This book is written for you. It will give you information, resources, options, and questions that you can think about on your own or discuss with girls your age.

Language

A very important aspect of *The JGirl's Guide* is language. Love of words and language is a cornerstone of Judaism. According to the Bible, "God said, 'Let there be light,' and there was light" (Genesis 1:3). The act of making words also made the world happen. This shows how important words are in the Jewish tradition. Over the centuries many commentaries have been written to further explain the words in the Bible. No word's meaning is taken for granted.

We have already used a few words that have very complicated meanings and may mean different things, depending on whom you ask. For example, *God, Judaism, Jewish,* and *the People Israel* mean one thing to a Reform Jew and another thing to an Orthodox Jew. Other examples of words that may not mean the same things to everybody are *matriarchy, patriarchy, feminist, girlfriend, boyfriend, family, partner, convert,* and *marriage.*

We have taken great care in choosing the words we use in *The JGirl's Guide.* Even so, we may unintentionally use words that make you feel left out or confused. It can be painful for someone who does not live with their parents to keep hearing about families where children always live with a mother and a father. Similarly, girls with health problems may be made uncomfortable by discussion of "a healthy body," a phrase they might not feel applies to them. Notice if we use words that make you feel like an outsider. What words would you use instead?

For example, take the word *God.* Did you wonder who or what God was when you were a small child? What do you think *God* means now? Has the meaning changed for you over the years? Do you think it could change again? Do you like to use Hebrew words for God, other words altogether, or no words at all?

Now a word about Hebrew and how we use it in this book. Hebrew is the language of the Bible and the language of Israel and the Jewish people today. It is the language that ties us together wherever we live. It is also the language of prayer. It includes many words that do not translate well into English. For example, in the biblical story of Creation, the name of the first human being is Adam. This word comes from the Hebrew root Alef-Dalet-Mem (A-D-M), which means "earth" or "ground." What the name Adam really means is "earth-thing," which makes sense because Adam was made out of earth. You would never know that from the English, however.

This book will contain many references to the Bible, which is the most important book in Jewish tradition. When Jews are called the People of the Book, the Bible is the book in question. The Bible includes a number of smaller books. When reference is made to a passage from the Bible, the name of the book is given along with the number of the relevant chapter and verse within that book. The story of the creation of light, for instance, appears in Genesis 1:3—that is, the third verse of the first chapter of the first book of the Bible.

The first books of the Bible are called the Five Books of Moses: Genesis (called *Bereshit* in Hebrew), Exodus *(Shmot),* Leviticus *(Vayikra),* Numbers *(Bemidbar),* and Deuteronomy *(D'varim).* These five books are also called the Torah, as is a handwritten scroll that contains these books. The Hebrew Bible, or Tanakh, also contains the works of the prophets and other writings such as Job, the Book of Ruth, and Chronicles. The word *Tanakh* comes from the first letter of the Hebrew words *Torah* (Instruction), *Nevi'im* (Prophets), and *K'tuvim* (Writings). The Hebrew Bible is what Christians call the Old Testament.

At the end of this book there is a glossary of Hebrew terms that will help you to understand Judaism better. You can skip over them or learn them. Judaism is very much tied to the Hebrew language, so we suggest you try to learn some Hebrew. If you already know a little Hebrew, we suggest you learn more.

Activities

In each chapter there are different sections that focus on an array of activities, skills, and Jewish knowledge. Following is a list of the different types of sections you will encounter. (These do not always appear in the order that they are listed here.)

Learn

In this section you will find the background and explanation of the mitzvah or *mitzvot* associated with each chapter. Included are ancient and modern Jewish sources, as well as current material from psychology, sociology, anthropology, and folklore to deepen your understanding. You will also learn Jewish concepts like *kol k'vodah bat melekh p'nimah*. These aren't *mitzvot*. They are values that guide Jewish practice and life.

M'korot (Jewish sources)

These are quotes and excerpts from ancient and contemporary Jewish sources that we hope you will use as inspiration for reflection and discussion.

Here is an example from an eighth-century commentary on the Book of Ecclesiastes in the Bible. Talking about the challenge of finding words of truth, the author of Ecclesiastes compares "words of the wise" to "nails well driven in" and "spurs" that poke an animal to make it move. The commentary, however, makes a surprising and very different comparison. It says:

> The words of the wise are like a young girl's ball. As a ball is tossed by hand without falling, so Moses received the Torah at Sinai and delivered it to Joshua, Joshua to the elders, the elders to the prophets, and the prophets delivered it to the Great Synagogue. —*Kohelet Rabbah* 12:11, on Ecclesiastes 12:11

What do you think of this comparison? What does it say about the commentary's view of young girls?

Discuss

In this section we encourage you to ask questions and form opinions. If you are reading the book with a group, you can explore your ideas together. Much of Jewish thought has been developed through discussion. In rabbinic times, sages argued and reasoned over the meanings of Jewish texts. We invite you to delve into the ideas in this book and make them your own.

Meet

Here we introduce you to Jewish women from all walks of life, all ages, all nationalities, and all backgrounds. Some are famous. Some could be your next-door neighbors or friends.

Write

Journal writing has been a way for girls and women to document their lives, confess secrets that could not be spoken anywhere else, and talk about sensitive issues like physical changes, relationships, and sexuality. There is rich material everywhere for writing, even in the routines of daily living.

Since 1947, reading *The Diary of Anne Frank* has often been a profound experience in self-affirmation for Jewish girls around the world. In it Anne Frank presents the daily and inner lives of a girl in hiding from the Nazis during the Holocaust.

We encourage you to keep a journal as you read this book. Keeping a journal can help you to clarify your goals and priorities, figure out your relationships, and learn more about yourself. We give you exercises for writing and using your journal. That way you can have a constant dialogue with the book and read back over what you have written to see how your ideas and viewpoints may have changed from the beginning of the book to the end.

Here is an exercise to warm you up. Think of something you wanted to do ever since you were a little girl but were always told, "You're too young. Wait until you grow up." Write about it or draw it in your journal. You can even talk to your journal. Anne Frank used this technique and called her journal "Kitty," as if she were writing to her best friend.

Pirkei Banot

The title of this section is adapted from the title of a famous book of wisdom called *Pirkei Avot,* which means "Sayings of the Fathers." In *Pirkei Banot,* which means "Sayings of the Daughters," we offer you quotes from girls and women, Jewish and non-Jewish, across the ages. Here is one by a Jewish teen in the 19th century about starting a journal:

> I begin tonight what I have long wished to begin, but something which I have never thought myself competent to do. Nor do I feel competent enough to do so now, but have at least common-sense enough to write simple facts and such things in general as I feel like writing. I will not pledge myself to write any stated time or any length, but have made up my mind to write when and how I feel inclined, as I am not going to let any, or at least very few persons see this nonsense: for such it must be if I write it.—Eliza Moses, May 1, 1861

Do It

This section suggests ways you can put into action the things you've learned about in each chapter. You've become familiar with the *mitzvot* described in the chapter; now it's up to you to experience them for yourself!

Think about It

These are additional points to consider about the topic in question, whether on your own, talking to a friend, or in a discussion with a larger group.

Resources

If you are interested in finding out more about a particular topic, you will find the names of books, magazines, films, videos, CDs, and websites at the back of this book.

Ahavat Israel (Love of the People Israel)

JGirls come in many shapes and sizes with diverse backgrounds, practices, and ideologies. Some wear tank tops and miniskirts. Others wear long skirts and long-sleeved shirts. Others wear jeans. On Friday nights and Saturday mornings, some JGirls go to synagogue while others go to *shul* and still others hang out with friends or do their homework. Some JGirls celebrate holidays with family and friends while others spend time in synagogue praying. Some JGirls do all these things.

One reason we wrote this book is that we love all Jews! This is actually a mitzvah known as *Ahavat Israel* (love of the People Israel). When you love someone, you don't think about whether that person belongs to this group or that group; whether they make their hot chocolate in a pan on the stove or in a mug in the microwave; or whether they prefer watching a sunset or a sunrise. You love that person for who he or she is inside. We welcome and embrace differences in the pages of this book and we hope that after you read it, you will have a greater sense of love, respect, and tolerance for your fellow JGirls.

In *The JGirl's Guide,* you will meet a variety of JGirls, each one unique in her own way. There is a midrash that states that all Jews, even those not yet born, were at Mount Sinai to receive the Torah. The midrash goes on to say that each one of them had his or her own interpretation of it. One beautiful thing about Judaism is that it leaves room for each individual to find their own Torah within the Torah we all share and within the practice of Jewish life. Judaism is colorful and multi-textured like the special coat of Joseph, whose story is told in the Book of Genesis.

One thing we would like you to take away from this book is *Ahavat Israel,* love and respect for your people. Although there is often disagreement about practice and belief in Judaism, the special bond within the Jewish community around the world is very important. We hope to create space within these pages for all JGirls to unite over their common experience of entering into the Jewish people.

Mitzvot:

Ve'ahavta l'reyakha kamokha (love
your neighbor as yourself);
Brit (covenant); G'milut chasadim
(acts of lovingkindness);
T'shuvah (repentance)

1 BEING A FRIEND

I love my friends,
but it's hard
to be a really good friend.

Dear JGirl,

Friends rock!

Whom do you hang out with at lunchtime? Who helps you to choose the best clothes at the mall? Who lends you a book she loved the minute she finishes it?

Your friends are the coolest people in your life these days. They may hang out with you at lunch, after school, and on weekends, or maybe you prefer to play soccer or tennis with them. Whatever you do, friends, both girls and boys, are probably a major part of your life.

Friends may also help you to deal with questions about relationships, dating, discomfort with your changing body, and fights with your parents. They are there to stick up for you when others gang up on you and to share some chocolate when you get a bad grade.

Sometimes, though, all the fun and friendship can get messed up. Your friends may do things that really upset you, like breaking promises, ignoring you, or telling your secrets. They may demand too much of your time or cancel plans with you to be with someone else. Inevitably teen friendship seems to include at least some fighting, frustration, and fury! Sometimes your negative feelings may pass. Sometimes you may realize that your best friend really isn't your best friend. Sometimes you may ask yourself, "What's the point of friends, anyway?"

This chapter will get you thinking about what it means to be a good friend and how to make your friendships even better.

Have fun!

Ali

WHAT ARE FRIENDS?

People define friendship differently, but all definitions have certain things in common: trust, loyalty, care, respect, understanding, similar values and shared interests, enjoying time together, and feeling comfortable around each other. In this chapter you will learn about being a good friend, to yourself and to others. You'll also get to know some famous friends in the Bible and make comparisons with your own friends. You'll come up with the essential ingredients of a good friendship, and you'll be able to test these.

One interpretation of the mitzvah *ve'ahavta l'reyakha kamokha* (love your neighbor as yourself, Leviticus 19:18) says that self-love is the basis of friendship. When you care enough about yourself, you make sure to stay healthy. You take care of your needs for love, mental stimulation, beauty, shelter, and understanding your place in the universe. You are a better friend when you are able to be good to yourself. Three aspects of the mitzvah of self-love are covenant, acts of lovingkindness, and repentance.

In Judaism the idea of a covenant, a contract between two responsible parties, is the foundation for a good friendship. In the Bible the covenant (Hebrew *brit*) between God and the Jewish People meant that God would protect them if they lived according to the Torah. Today, a covenant means that two or more people agree to do or not to do something specific. Friendship is a covenant between two or more people to be good friends to each other, however they define it.

DISCUSS

Here are three signs of covenant that occur in the Bible, followed by questions for you to think about and/or discuss.

- **Rainbow:** a sign of God's promise, made after the great flood, never to bring destruction on the world again. "When I bring clouds over the earth, and the bow appears in the clouds, I will remember My covenant between Me and you and every living creature among all flesh, so that the waters shall never again become a flood to destroy all flesh" (Genesis 9:14–15).

   Question: When you and your friends get angry and frustrated with each other, can you find a way to fix things and renew your friendship? Can you appreciate the differences between you and your friends? Differences can actually enrich your relationship, even though it may be difficult to accept that you and your friends do not always think or feel the same way.

- **Shabbat:** a weekly reminder of the covenant between God and the Jewish People. "The Israelite people shall keep the Sabbath, observing the Sabbath throughout the ages as a covenant for all time: It shall be a sign for all time between Me and the people of Israel" (Exodus 31:16–17).

   Question: Do you and your friends have a way of reaffirming your friendship on a regular basis?

- **The Torah:** the collected wisdom and way of life of the Jewish People, a gift given by God. "If you listen to these laws and keep them and do them, *Adonai* your God will keep the covenant and the lovingkindness sworn to your ancestors" (Deuteronomy 7:12).

    Question: Friendship is something you get from, because you give to. How do you understand this?

PIRKEI BANOT

"My friends know things about me without my having to tell them, just by my attitude and face. I can tell them anything and they're not going to judge me. I can't go for that long without talking to them. We know almost everything about each other."
—Lauren, 15

"One of the most important characteristics [of a friendship] should be trust. A good friend must be trustworthy. They should care about you, love you, listen to you, help you mend a broken heart, share experiences with you. A good friend is considerate, is always there for you, and is someone you can count on. They should be nice, friendly, interesting, and supportive. There are so many things that make up a good friend, but a really important thing is loving you for who you are." —Ariela, 13

Do It

Who Is Your Friend?

Write 10 points describing your friend. These can include name, favorite music, foods, activities, hobbies, and talents. Consider why you are friends and what you like most about this person.

Share your descriptions with your friend if you like.

MEET

David and Jonathan

A sincere friendship is based on intimacy, privacy, honor, respect, continual cultivation, giving and taking, and all-around care for one another. In the Bible, the story of David and Jonathan exemplifies the Jewish ideal of friendship. Jonathan was the son of King Saul. When Saul realized that David, a humble shepherd, was a far better warrior than he and was destined to be the next king of Israel, he became jealous and decided to kill David. Jonathan had to make a choice between his father and David, who was his friend. He sacrificed his relationship with his father and chose loyalty to his friend (1 Samuel 18:1–4). Jonathan helped David to flee and thus saved his life.

What does it mean that they were such good friends? Did Jonathan call on David every 10 minutes? Did they spend all of their free time together? Did Jonathan constantly shower David with compliments? No. They were called good friends because they loved each other and would have done anything for one another. When he learned of Jonathan's death, David said, "Jonathan, my brother, you were most dear to me" (2 Samuel 1:26).

Naomi and Ruth

In the biblical period of the Judges there was a famine in Israel. One wealthy and prominent family in Bethlehem, from the tribe of Judah, was able to escape. Elimelech, his wife, Naomi, and his two sons, Chilion and Machlon, packed up and took off to the land of Moab.

When they arrived in Moab, life improved. Elimelech continued with his business, Naomi was delighted in their new home, and the boys assimilated to their environments. Chilion married a Moabite woman named Ruth, and Machlon married a Moabite woman named Orpah. Life was good for Elimelech and his family: they had a large house, plenty of food, and good health.

Then things took a turn for the worse. Elimelech, Machlon, and Chilion all died. Naomi's daughters-in-law remained with her throughout the period of mourning. Soon Naomi decided that it was time for her to return to her old home in Bethlehem. At first both her daughters-in-law insisted that they would return with her, but when Naomi explained that she had nothing to offer them, Orpah went back to her own family.

Ruth, however, insisted on staying with her mother-in-law. When Naomi told Ruth she was free to go home, Ruth said, "Do not urge me to leave you, to go back from following you—for wherever you go, I will go; where you lodge, I will lodge. Your people are my people, and your God is my God. Where you will die, I will die, and there I will be buried" (Ruth 1:16–17).

It must have been very difficult for Ruth to leave her homeland and journey to another land with an entirely different religion. For Ruth was not only being loyal to Naomi. By saying, "Your people are my people and your God is my God," she became Jewish.

When they arrived in Israel, a wealthy and kind landowner named Boaz, a cousin of Naomi's, allowed Ruth to gather barley in his fields during the harvest. (This is a right guaranteed by the Torah to the poor, to widows, and to orphans.) Ruth worked in the sweltering sun every day, and one day Boaz invited her to eat with him. When Naomi noticed his growing interest in her daughter-in-law, she encouraged Ruth to let him know she was available for marriage.

Ruth did so, and Boaz and Ruth married and had a son named Oved, who was the grandfather of King David, the greatest king of Israel. According to Jewish tradition, Ruth and Boaz merited such a remarkable descendant because of their caring behavior, toward each other and toward others. A simple but beautiful explanation of the purpose of the Book of Ruth was given by Rabbi Zeira, who said: "This scroll tells us nothing either of ritual purity or impurity, either of things prohibited or permitted. Why then was it written? To teach how great is the reward of those who perform acts of kindness" (Ruth Rabbah 2:14).

DISCUSS

- Can you recall a time when you became friends with someone unexpectedly?
- Do you think girls have a different kind of friendship with other girls than they have with boys? How so?
- How would you define loyalty? If a friend tells you a secret and you refrain from telling anyone, are you being loyal? If you hear someone speaking badly about your friend, can you still be a loyal friend if you don't speak up to defend her?
- What acts of kindness did Ruth and Jonathan perform? Can you think of a time in your own life when you acted like Ruth or Jonathan?

LEARN

Ruth and Naomi and David and Jonathan exemplify a major pillar of Jewish belief, a concept called *g'milut chasadim,* which means doing acts of kindness. *Pirkei Avot* (1:2) says that the world rests on three things: Torah, service to God, and acts of lovingkindness. Examples of *g'milut chasadim* are welcoming guests into your home, helping someone in need, and greeting people kindly rather than harshly. Jewish tradition explains that just as God performs acts of kindness, so should we: "Blessed are You, God, who performs acts of lovingkindness," we say in the daily prayers.

A separate but related mitzvah is *bikkur cholim,* visiting the sick.

What is lovingkindness, and how do these two biblical pairs show us how to do it?

The Hebrew term for the quality of lovingkindness is *chesed;* performing acts of lovingkindness is *g'milut chasadim.* Helping someone with no other motivation than being there for them is an example of *g'milut chasadim.* Ruth accompanied Naomi because she didn't want her mother-in-law to be alone and suffer. She put aside her own needs to be with her birth family, to remarry and have children. Jonathan put David's needs ahead of his own, even risking his life to save him.

Do you think acting as unselfishly as Ruth and Jonathan did is possible today?

Do It

Random Acts of *Chesed*

Sunday
- Offer to help a parent with chores around the house.
- Take flowers to a neighbor, friend, or relative.
- Smile at one person you don't know.

Monday
- Wish a parent, sibling, bus driver, or friend at school a good morning.
- Call a grandparent, an aunt, an uncle, or a cousin to say hello.
- Recycle your drink bottle or can at lunch.

Tuesday
- Make your bed without being asked.
- Read a story to your younger sibling.
- Sit with the "new girl" at lunch.

Wednesday
- Thank your teacher for something during school.

- Send someone who is feeling sad a humorous greeting card.
- Wish all the members of your household "sweet dreams."

Thursday

- Compliment your friend on an accomplishment.
- If someone was absent from school, call her and tell her the homework she missed.
- Bring the recycling box back to your neighbor.

Friday

- Call a friend to wish her or him "Shabbat shalom."
- Water the plants in your house without being asked or reminded to do it.
- Set the table for dinner.

Saturday

- Take your younger sibling for a walk.
- Spend some time with a friend or relative who is sick or lonely.
- Plan a special outing with a family member.

PIRKEI BANOT

Menschlikhkeit, the quality of being a *mensch* (Yiddish for "a good person"), is a "cousin" of *chesed*. This story from Itka Zygmuntowicz, who grew up in Poland and came to the United States in 1953, illustrates this principle. Itka was a prisoner in three concentration camps and the only person in her family to survive the Holocaust.

> I remember once I came home crying bitterly because, as I was walking home from school, a group of non-Jewish kids I did not even know attacked me. When I came home, my mother asked me, "Why are you crying, Itka?"

And I told her. She tried to comfort me. Later, she looked at me, and she asked me, "What did you do, my child?" And I said, "Nothing." And my mother said with assurance, "Well then, you have nothing to cry about. Your *menschlikhkeit* does not depend on how others treat you but on how you treat others."

DISCUSS

Use any of the following quotes that inspire you to start a discussion about friendship with a friend, parent, sibling, or classmate.

"Walking with a friend in the dark is better than walking alone in the light." —Helen Keller

"A person who loves a friend cannot stand by and watch that friend be beaten and insulted. The person would come to the friend's aid." —Rabbi Moshe Chaim Luzzato, *Mesilat Yesharim* 19:17

"Friendship is like a heart-flooding feeling that can happen to any two people who are caught up in the act of being themselves, and who like what they see." —Letty Cottin Pogrebin

"The greatest good you can do for another is not just to share your riches, but to reveal to him his own." —Benjamin Disraeli

PROBLEMS WITH FRIENDS

LEARN

The Hebrew word *t'shuvah* means "turning." It's what Jews do every Rosh Hashanah and Yom Kippur when we "turn" our attention back to the year that has just passed. Looking back on the year, we see things that we might wish we had done differently, things we wish we had or hadn't said, things we would change in our behavior. We take stock and try to figure out how we might "turn the situation around" and do better next time. *T'shuvah* means the ability to feel shame and remorse for something we have done, to change our ways, to "turn back" after a quarrel and apologize to someone, asking for forgiveness *(slichah)* and pardon *(m'chilah)*.

With a friend, there are always opportunities for *t'shuvah* because friendship is dynamic; it is always changing. This is the nature of human beings and their relationships. Sometimes we are both on the same wavelength; at other times we can hurt each other to the core. Friends, like all people, are usually not the same as time passes. If they were, the friendship could get pretty boring!

What Are the Arguments About?

Do these sound familiar? Look at this list and see how many of these friendship trouble spots ring true for you.

- Jealousy over possessions, other friends, grades, parents
- Divulging secrets
- Breaking plans
- Talking behind each other's back
- Lying to each other
- Asking one to lie for the other

Resolving Arguments

"One who covers a transgression seeks love, but one who repeats a matter separates close friends." —Proverbs 17:9

Arguments and disagreements with your friends don't necessarily signal the end of your friendship. In fact, how you handle a disagreement can be a valuable test of a friendship. Friends who are able to disagree about things and still be friends will be able to grow together. Some friendships, however, cannot withstand disagreement or differences of opinion, and these friends might need to go in different directions, or the relationship might need to change significantly.

Here are some tips on "making up" with your friends:

- Talking loudly or crying will prevent you from accurately conveying your feelings. Instead, try to speak calmly. If you feel too upset to talk about it, you can always communicate your feelings in a letter or e-mail.
- If you have a problem with a specific person, confront that person directly. This requires courage and has to be done with good manners, but you won't solve the problem unless you speak to the relevant person. Talking *about* someone to another only makes things worse. "Do not go talebearing among your people" (Leviticus 19:16).
- Always be specific as to why are you are upset and emphasize your own feelings. For example, "I felt embarrassed in front of the entire lunch table after what you said today!" Saying how you felt will release the anger. "You shall not take revenge or bear a grudge" (Leviticus 19:18).
- Listen and don't interrupt. If you want respect when you are talking, you must give the same respect to your friends.

- Attacking and name-calling are counterproductive; they will only prolong the argument and deepen hurt feelings.
- Don't tell others to dislike a former friend. You wouldn't want someone to do this to you.

PIRKEI BANOT

"One of the most difficult friendship problems I've ever encountered is knowing when to tell a secret—when a friend is in trouble and confides in you, and you know you need to tell someone. It's so difficult to consciously break a friend's trust, even though you may know you're doing the right thing. The most important thing to remember in a situation like that is that, despite whatever anger your friend throws at you at the time, you're doing the right thing for her." —Rachel, 17

Cliques

Cliques are the underside of friendship. The dictionary defines *clique* as a "small, exclusive group of people." Everyone has had experience with a clique, either being in one or being left out of one. Human beings naturally form groups to accomplish tasks, to support each other, or to learn together. Your family is your first group experience. For better or worse, you are automatically included in your family when you are born or adopted.

Obviously, you are not born into your group of friends. Friendship is a matter of choice. People may come into and go from your group as they wish, or people may be allowed in one at a time and only if they fit certain requirements of the group.

People form cliques to gain a sense of control and power. Members of a clique can accept or reject new members. Sometimes, in order to feel better about themselves members single out someone to reject. This is called *scapegoating*. The term comes from the

Torah. In biblical times, the Israelites observed Yom Kippur by projecting their sins onto a goat that would then be sent into the wilderness—hence a "scapegoat." The people were then forgiven of the sins that they had put on this goat (Leviticus 16:9–10).

People come up with many "reasons" to scapegoat other human beings. As Jews, we should be extremely sensitive to this, because throughout history we have been scapegoated—for the death of Jesus, the Black Death, and many other tragedies. We have been singled out, libeled, shunned, and degraded because people projected their problems onto Jews. The Holocaust is the ultimate example of this cruel behavior to date.

Cliques use scapegoats to make it clear who is "in" the group and who is "out." Under pressure to behave according to what is acceptable to the group, people often scapegoat others because they are "smart" or "stupid," "confident" or "too quiet," "good-looking" or "ugly." In the area of friendship, most of us have been guilty at one time or another of scapegoating others.

Learning how to handle being included in or excluded from a group is a major step on the road to maturity. It can help to ask older siblings, cousins, parents, teachers, and coaches how they handled cliques.

THINK ABOUT IT

Take some time to think about these questions:

- How do you deal with the cliques you've encountered?
- Do you have a group of friends who only hang out with each other and no one else? If yes, how do you feel about being "inside" this group? How do you feel about those "outside" your group?
- Are you friendly with different types of people who do not belong to any one group? Why or why not?

PIRKEI BANOT

"I do not know what's wrong, but something is definitely wrong! I would like to know whether there are any other girls in this whole world like myself. I am anxious, crazy to learn, but at the same time want to go out and have a good time; true, I am not quite so crazy for the boys as the majority of girls are and when in company with them I am quite shy.... I am continually getting myself into embarrassing situations; embarrassing to myself alone, yet they bother me for 24 hours after." —Jennie Franklin, November 26, 1890

WRITE

This is a good time to use your journal to explore what friendship means to you. Here are some questions and suggestions to start you thinking, but don't limit yourself to these ideas. Wherever your writing takes you will be valuable.

- What does friendship mean to you?
- What importance does friendship have in your life?
- Who is your oldest friend? How have you managed to stay friends so long?
- What do you look for in a friend now that is different from what you used to look for in a friend?
- Have you had a problem with a friend? How did you solve it?
- Write a poem about friendship.
- Write a letter to a friend. You may choose to show her the letter or not. Tell her what you appreciate about your friendship; tell her ways in which you would like to change your friendship.
- Would you like to make a new friend? What would that person be like? Do you know him or her already? Are you ready to try to become their friend? How can you make it happen?

FINAL WORDS

Now you know the three pillars of friendship, *brit, g'milut chasadim,* and *t'shuvah.* These pillars support you in your quest for meaningful, positive, healthy relationships. You have the tools to be a better friend, to yourself and to others. Consider this: You are your own best friend. No one will ever know you better than you know yourself. Because you are no longer a "little girl," you can take on the adult task of getting to know yourself. Being your own best friend will let you become a friend to others. In a story called "Happiness," Anne Frank wrote the following about one of her characters: "I haven't found happiness yet," she said, "but I found something else—someone who understands me."

2 BEING A DAUGHTER

I love my parents,
but do I need to
honor them, too?

Dear JGirl,

One minute they're making your lunch for school. The next, they're asking you to change your clothes for something more "appropriate." Later on they give you a kiss and wish you a nice day. Although they may let you go to the movies with your friends on the weekends, they insist on an early curfew, no negotiations.

Your relationship with your parents may be changing these days for a number of reasons. Not only do parents have to adjust to your new interests and energy (you are bursting with hormones, ideas, sexuality, peer pressure, and many other things), you are going to have to change as well, in order to meet them halfway. While you insist on a later curfew, more privacy, and boys in your room, they may insist on the opposite.

One of the most important mitzvot *is honoring your parents— it's so important, it's one of the Ten Commandments. How do you do this in a world that is telling you that parents are old-fashioned and overprotective, that parents can't understand you, that parents don't have a clue what life is about, that parents went to school so long ago they've forgotten what it's like?*

The way in which you and your parents communicate these days may be more challenging than when you were younger and more dependent on them. You are changing, and they are learning to deal with your changes. One of the hardest things about becoming a teenager is learning how to adjust your relationship with your parents. Although you might still love them deeply, you might feel that they don't understand you or why you get frustrated with them. Yet you might also feel that you are growing closer with them and that your experience of the teen years is going fairly smoothly. The main thing is to keep talking about it all—together.

When you feel as though your parents don't understand you, remember that there is an age gap. They still see you as their baby girl, although you might see yourself as an independent person now. This struggle has been going on since parents and children have existed. You want more privacy, independence, and freedom. They want to let you have all these things, but they worry about your safety, your feelings, and your future.

Parents are also there to be your guides when the going gets tough. Remember, they too went through puberty, crushes, high school, and confusion! In this chapter there are suggestions on how to stay close to your parents and have a meaningful relationship with them while you all navigate the bumpy road to independence.

Good luck!

Ali

THE FIFTH COMMANDMENT

LEARN

The commandment to honor your parents is taken very seriously in Judaism. The fifth of the Ten Commandments is *Kabed et avikha ve'et imekha* (Honor your father and your mother) (Exodus 20:12). The first five commandments all have to do with relations between God and humans; the second five have to do with relations between humans and humans. One might think that the command to honor one's parents would be part of the latter, but it isn't. Honoring your parents is included in the first category because God is considered to be the third partner, with the parents, in making children. When you honor your parents, therefore, you also honor God (Babylonian Talmud, *Kiddushin* 30b and *Niddah* 31a). This is hard for young people to do. The Jerusalem Talmud (*Peah* 1:1) says, "Honoring a father and mother is the most difficult mitzvah."

Every form of Judaism considers the family unit to be essential in supporting the Jewish People. In traditional Judaism, parents are considered to be the earthly embodiment of what God is to humans: As God is the Power that creates us, the Power to which we owe gratitude for our lives, so too are our parents on the earthly plane. If we dishonor our parents, we dishonor God, the Source of our existence.

Because you and your parents have different needs, it is crucial to search for ways to enable both of you to deal with change. As you progress from being a child to becoming an adult, you change the way you see your parents. As a child you probably saw your parents mostly as providers. As an adult you will be able to see them as people who gave you life. You will begin to recognize the respect and honor that they deserve.

As you are changing your view of your parents, they are changing their view of you. They will start to see you as an individual, someone who is still dependent on them yet learning how to be

self-sufficient. In this chapter you will find ways to show your gratitude and appreciation.

JEWISH MOTHERS

MEET
Ima (Mother) and *Imahot* (Matriarchs)

Each of us has a personal mother, a woman who gave birth to us and
raised us. Some of us may have more than one mother—one who
gave birth to us *and* one who raised us. Eve, the first mother on
earth, was called *em kol chai* (mother of all that is alive). As Jews, we
also have four ancestral mothers, the women who gave birth to the
Jewish people. They are Sarah, Rebecca, Rachel, and Leah. The
Midrash sometimes includes two other women—Bilhah and Zilpah,
who were the wives of Jacob and the mothers of Jewish tribes as well
(see, e.g., *Numbers Rabbah* 12:17).

Here is a family tree of the matriarchs and patriarchs.

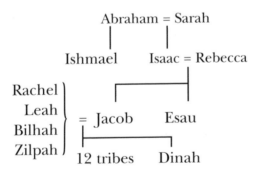

Following are descriptions of the four matriarchs. In Hebrew
the word for "matriarch" is the same as the word for biological
mother, *ima*.

Sarah Imeynu *(Sarah, Our Mother)*

Sarah's name means "princess." She became the wife of Abraham, the founder of monotheism, although she was his brother's daughter. (Such marriages were common at the time.) Sarah went with Abraham on his mission to leave his birthplace and go to a new land to start a new people. Together they spread the message of One God.

Sarah is known for speaking her mind and saying what bothered her. When she could not have a child, she told Abraham to have a child with their maid, Hagar, and "Abraham listened to the voice of Sarah" (Genesis 16:2). Hagar's child was named Ishmael.

Meanwhile, God finally promised Sarah, at age 90, a child. When she heard this, Sarah "laughed within herself, saying 'After I am grown old shall I have pleasure, my lord being old also?'" (Genesis 18:12). She gave birth to Isaac, who soon became his half-brother's rival. Sarah thought that Hagar was disrespectful to her, so she convinced Abraham to send Hagar and Ishmael off into the wilderness.

Later, Sarah woke up one morning to find that Abraham and Isaac had left the house early. At that moment Abraham, at God's command, was preparing to sacrifice his son on Mt. Moriah. In the end, however, an angel prevented him from doing so. According to a midrash, when Abraham and Isaac returned home, Sarah had died—from the shock of hearing that Isaac was being sacrificed.

Rivka Imeynu *(Rebecca, Our Mother)*

Abraham sent his servant Eliezer from Canaan to find a wife for Isaac in Mesopotamia, the land of his birth. Eliezer brought camels, jewelry, and other gifts for the woman he expected to find. He devised the following test to make sure he chose the finest wife for his master's son: He would wait with his camels by the village well. When a girl came down to the well to fetch water for her family, he would ask her for a drink of water from her pitcher. The first girl to say, "Certainly I shall give you water, and I will water your animals as well" would merit the hand of Isaac in marriage.

When Rebecca came down to the well to fetch water and Eliezer asked her for a drink, she offered some to him and also volunteered to give water to his camels. Eliezer knew then that she was the girl destined to be Isaac's wife. He made her father an offer of marriage on behalf of Isaac. Rebecca herself agreed to leave her homeland and go to Canaan. Isaac brought Rebecca into his mother's tent, and they were married. He loved her, and she was able to comfort him after the death of his mother, Sarah.

Like Sarah, Rebecca was infertile for a time; then she gave birth to twins. During her pregnancy, she could feel that something was wrong. When she asked God what was going on, God said, "Two nations are in your womb. One people shall be stronger than the other people, and the elder shall serve the younger" (Genesis 25:23).

When the twins were older, Jacob, the younger, persuaded Esau, the elder, to sell him his birthright as the firstborn for a bowl of lentil stew. Rebecca, who favored Jacob, then disguised him as Esau in order to receive his father's blessing. Isaac was old and blind by then, and was not sure whom he was blessing. He said, upon touching Jacob, "The voice is the voice of Jacob, but the hands are the hands of Esau" (Genesis 27:22). Isaac gave Jacob the blessing of the firstborn. When Esau learned what happened, he was very bitter. Isaac too was angry, for he favored Esau. Jacob paid for his deceit, by being deceived by others for the rest of his life.

Rachel Imeynu (Rachel, Our Mother)

Jacob left home because Rebecca feared for his life after he tricked Esau. Jacob traveled to Rebecca's homeland, where her brother,

Laban, still lived. There Jacob happened upon his cousin Rachel at the town well, and he instantly fell in love with her. Rachel had an older sister, Leah. It was the custom for the older sister to be married first, but when Jacob asked for Rachel's hand in marriage, Laban agreed, on one condition—that Jacob would work for seven years to become her husband. At the wedding, however, Laban switched the sisters (the bride wore a veil over her face)—just as Jacob had once been switched with his brother. Much to his surprise and dismay, Jacob found himself married to Leah. Nevertheless, he loved Rachel so much that he agreed to work for another seven years for her, and a week after he married Leah, he married Rachel. (Polygamy, or having more than one wife, was common at the time, and it was not unusual for a man's wives to be sisters.)

Leah immediately began bearing children, but Rachel did not. Rachel prayed to God and asked Jacob to pray for her, too. Years later, she gave birth to Joseph (who became Jacob's favorite son), and then she died giving birth to Benjamin, the youngest of the sons of Jacob. In the meantime, Rachel and Leah's maidservants, Bilhah and Zilpah, each had two sons by Jacob. (See Genesis 30.)

At the tomb of Rachel today, just outside Bethlehem, people come to receive blessings. Women, especially those experiencing infertility and problems in pregnancy, come to the tomb to pray.

Leah Imeynu *(Leah, Our Mother)*

Leah was an unappreciated wife. Even though she was able to bear more children than Rachel, she was less loved by Jacob, and her children were not as cherished by their father. Leah is known for her eyes, which are described as *rakot* in Hebrew. That could mean "weak," "tender," or "delicate." A midrash says that her eyes became that way from crying.

DISCUSS

- Rebecca, Isaac, and Jacob each had a favorite son. What do you think about parents having favorite children?
- Was Rebecca's reason for changing the order of things a good one? What would you have done in her situation?
- What kinds of things do parents do to protect their children or promote their success? What do your parents do? What would you do if you were a parent?

M'KOROT

Kadya Molodowsky (1894–1975) was a Polish poet who wrote in Yiddish. This poem, from a collection of her works translated by Kathryn Hellerstein, entitled *Paper Bridges,* refers to the four Mothers—Sarah, Rebecca, Rachel, and Leah—as guardians of certain kinds of earthly women.

> For poor brides who were servant girls,
> Mother Sara draws forth from dim barrels
> And pitchers sparkling wine.
> Mother Sara carries with both hands
> A full pitcher to whom it is decreed.
> And for streetwalkers
> Dreaming of white wedding shoes,
> Mother Sara bears clear honey
> In small saucers
> To their tired mouths.
> For high-born brides now poor,
> Who blush to bring patched wash
> Before their mother-in-law,
> Mother Rebecca leads camels

Laden with white linen.
And when darkness spreads before their feet,
And all the camels kneel on the ground to rest,
Mother Rebecca measures linen ell by ell
From her fingers to her golden bracelet.
For those whose eyes are tired
From watching the neighborhood children,
And whose hands are thin from yearning
For a soft small body
And for the rocking of a cradle,
Mother Rachel brings healing leaves
Discovered on distant mountains,
And comforts them with a quiet word:
At any hour God may open the sealed womb.
For those who cry at night in lonely beds,
And have no one to share their sorrow,
Who talk to themselves with parched lips,
To them, Mother Leah comes quietly,
Her eyes covered with her pale hands.

WRITE

Write a piece of your own about Sarah, Rebecca, Rachel, and Leah. As you can see, each of the four Mothers has a distinct personality and life story. Each one speaks to a different life situation.

Which Mother do you relate to the most? Write a letter to her and tell her about something that comes to your mind. It could be a problem, an insight, a question, or a secret. It should be something you think she could respond to with her own wisdom and compassion.

Make up a story about one of the Mothers, something that you wonder about her. Let this story fill in the gaps in her story as told in the Bible.

PARENTS TODAY

THINK ABOUT IT

Before looking at Jewish sources on honoring parents, let's consider what *honor* means.

- Who in society is honored?
- Consider the following people and whether or how they are honored: the queen of England, when she makes a state visit to another country; the president of the United States; your favorite pop star; a firefighter who saves all the people in a house that is on fire.
- What does a person have to do to be honored?
- Should a person be honored for just being him- or herself?
- Is there anyone at school whom you honor?
- Whom else, besides your parents, do you honor in your life?
- How can you honor someone?
- When the Torah commands people to honor their parents, does it refer to loving them, or only to obligations, such as helping them with chores and being polite, or feeding and clothing them when they can't do this for themselves? Is it equivalent to *respect?*
- What do your parents mean to you? How can you show them how you feel?
- What word would you use to describe the ideal relationship between a child and a parent?

Let's also consider what *parents* means. Today, there are traditional families that include a mother, a father, and children, and there are nontraditional families such as grandparents and children; single parents and children; adoptive parents and adoptive children; foster parents and foster children; stepfather, mother, and children; father, stepmother, and children; and same-sex parents and children. Whenever you see *parents* in this chapter, it means adults in the parental role; they are not necessarily the biological parents of the child. According to *halakhah*, the legal code of traditional Judaism, people who assume a parental role with a child whose biological parents are not able to take care of him or her are to be honored just like biological parents.

M'KOROT

Look at these selections from Jewish sources and consider how they do or do not affect you today.

"Honor your father and your mother." —Exodus 20:12

"Honoring your parents is the most difficult mitzvah." —Jerusalem Talmud, *Peah* 1:1

"God accounts honor shown to parents as though it were shown to God, and, conversely, the neglect of honoring parents is regarded as an insult to God." —*Mechilta* on Exodus 20:12

To these positive commandments, Maimonides adds three negative ones: not to curse your father or mother, not to strike your father or mother, and not to rebel against the authority of your father or mother (*Sefer Hamitzvot*, Book 2, Nos. 318, 319, and 195). A separate but related mitzvah is to show deference to the elderly (Leviticus 19:32).

WRITE

Keep a journal for a week in which you record all your interactions with your parents, writing down what took place. How does the mitzvah of *kibud av va'em* enter into it? Discuss what happened with your parents. Come up with ways in which you could improve in honoring and respecting your parents.

Now make a list of things that you know upset your parents, then list ways you can rectify the situation. Following are three examples:

1. When I don't do my homework. *Make a conscious effort to do homework without being nagged.*

2. When I spend too much time on the phone or instant messaging. *Set time limits and plan activities.*

3. When I fight with my sibling(s). *Try to work out disagreements without raising my voice.*

Finally, list ten things your parents do for you:

1. They brought me into this world (or adopted me).

2. _____

3. _____

4. _____

5. _____

6. _____

7. _____

8. _____

9. _____

10. _____

Ways I Can Honor My Parents

1. Clean my room
2. Take out the garbage without being asked
3. Help with preparation of dinner and cleanup afterwards
4. Make them breakfast in bed
5. Write a letter or poem of appreciation
6. Help my sister or brother with homework
7. Take clear and polite phone messages for them
8. Speak to them in an appreciative and respectful manner
9. Wish them a good day before I leave for school
10. Invite them to play a board game or cards

Getting to Know Your Parents

The better you know your parents, the easier it can be to honor and respect them. Here are questions to get you going on a fascinating interview with your parents. There are probably many events, people, and travels they have experienced about which you know nothing or very little. Your parents had a whole life before you came into it.

Set aside time to find out about this, if they are willing. Plan on one to two hours, and make sure you won't have any interruptions. Take notes or have a tape recorder going. You may even want to videotape your parents as you interview them. Include ways in which they honored *their* parents. How have times changed? However you decide to document the interview, make sure you keep it in a safe place. This interview will be a piece of family history that you might want to take out again and again. Eventually, you might want to show it to your children. You might even be starting a family tradition!

Interview Questions: You don't have to stick to these questions; they are just ideas to get you started. You might also want to use family photos and special keepsakes that are important to your parents to get them talking.

- Where were they born? If outside the North America, what was their immigration experience like?
- Did they go to high school, college, graduate school?
- What are their occupations? What do their jobs entail?
- What are their hobbies and interests?
- Who are their best friends? Who were their friends while they were growing up?
- What is unique about them?
- What do they like best about being a Jewish woman or man?
- What part of Judaism most appeals to them?
- Did they have a bat or bar mitzvah, and what was it like?
- What do they think is the reason to have a bat mitzvah?
- What do they want you to get out of your experience as a bat mitzvah?
- What historical events have they lived through, and what are their thoughts about them?

Do It

One good way to improve your relationship with your parents is to engage in fulfilling a mitzvah with them, such as the mitzvah of *tzedakah* (charity). *Tzedakah* can be a way to work together for a cause that goes far beyond you and your parents. Here are some suggestions for family *tzedakah* projects:

- Volunteer at a soup kitchen.
- Sort through old clothes and give them to needy families.

- Prepare a Shabbat meal for a needy family and deliver it anonymously.
- Set aside a *tzedakah* box for one cause and put coins in the box once a week (it is traditional to do this just before Shabbat begins).
- Organize a cleanup of your neighborhood. Pick up trash in the street and dispose of it properly.

DISCUSS

Think about the meaning of love and honor. Look them up in the dictionary if that would help. Discuss with your parents why we are commanded to honor our parents but are not commanded to love them.

WHEN HONORING PARENTS IS A PROBLEM

There are times when you cannot honor your parents. If you are being emotionally, physically, or sexually abused by a parent, how could you possibly honor him or her? Protecting your parents from being found out by your teachers, relatives, and friends because you feel you must honor them is not going to help anyone. No child deserves to be abused, and it is imperative to reach out for help.

If you are being abused and need help, here are some options for you to consider. Find an adult you can trust to talk about it with: a teacher, the parent of a friend, a rabbi, a counselor, or a doctor. Find a safe place for shelter if you need to leave your home. Call Jewish Family and Children's Services in your community.

FINAL WORDS

Someday you might be a parent. If that happens, how do you think you'll look back on this time in your life?

The struggles you are experiencing are important—and even valuable. Together with your parents, you are working on the task of growing up. This work takes into account their experiences as teens along with yours. Your parents brought you into the world and are raising you. If you were adopted or do not live with your birth parents, the adults who care for you brought you into their lives and are raising you. Up until now you have been their responsibility completely; that is changing. You are gaining responsibility and authority over your own life, but it doesn't happen in one day. You will work for many years to become a fulfilled, productive adult, a person who can make a living by honest work and give something back to the world. You and your parents are preparing for the time when you leave their care and go out into the world on your own.

3 EATING

I like to eat,
but I think
about food a lot.

Dear JGirl,

Will it be a burger and fries for lunch, a slice of pizza and a cola, or tuna on whole-grain bread and bottled water? Do you enjoy sitting in front of the TV with a bag of chips and a soft drink? Is your favorite snack a candy bar or grapes?

A new surge of hunger is typical for a girl your age, since your body is changing rapidly. You may also feel more tired, moodier, and grumpier than you used to feel. Believe it or not, all of these new-found feelings are strongly connected to nutrition. Because your bones are growing, you need more calcium. Because your energy level is changing, you need more protein and healthy carbohydrates. Because you are becoming a woman, your body requires many more minerals and vitamins than you needed as a child.

Besides feeling different physically, you may also change your attitudes toward food as you move into and through your teens. Whereas once you could gobble down ten chocolate chip cookies and not feel stuffed, as you become older you may begin to have a different relationship with food.

In this chapter you will find healthy ways to adjust to the new needs of your body. Today you are being bombarded with all sorts of negative messages about diet, weight, and body image. There is a positive way of looking at food, however: It's what keeps us alive and healthy. It protects us from disease and keeps us energized throughout the day. Food is not something to take for granted. You can feel your relationship with the earth as you eat, if you take the time to be aware of it. The focus of this chapter will be on developing a positive relationship with food and thus a positive relationship with your body.

Part of being Jewish means eating, talking, and celebrating—and sometimes not eating, praying, and mourning. Most of our holidays contain some aspect of feasting or fasting. From potato latkes on Chanukah to matzah on Passover to cheese bourekas *on Shavuot, food is a major part of Jewish celebration. Keeping kosher is a Jewish practice that can help you respect your food.*

B'teyavon! (To a healthy appetite!)

Ali

JEWISH FOOD

LEARN

What does food mean to you? Food has different meanings at different times of the year, in different cultures, and in different families. It relates to the following:

- Basic survival
- Nutrition
- Celebration of a particular holiday
- Hospitality and the nurturing qualities of the one who provides and prepares meals
- Preparation as an art form
- A means of passing down traditions and beliefs at meals and during their preparation
- Pleasure
- Denial

The following list shows how particular foods are associated with each holiday in the Jewish year:

- **Rosh Hashanah (New Year)**
  Apples and honey (sweetness for the coming year)
  Pomegranate (fertility, symbolized by many seeds)
  Fish head (the "head" of the year)
- **Yom Kippur (Day of Atonement)**
  No food (to "afflict" our bodies on this day of repentance)
- **Sukkot (Harvest Festival; 40 Years in the Wilderness)**
  Wheat, barley, olives, pomegranates, grapes, figs, and dates (the seven species of the Land of Israel)
- **Simchat Torah (Joy of Torah)**
  Candy (sweetness of Torah)
- **Chanukah (Festival of Lights; Maccabee victory over Syrian Greeks)**
  Potato latkes, doughnuts (fried foods to commemorate the oil that lasted for eight days)
  Chocolate coins (Chanukah *gelt*)
- **Tu B'Shvat (15th of Shvat, New Year for Trees)**
  Fruits that come from trees, like carob, oranges, dates, and olives (Some fruits, such as strawberries, pineapples,

grapes, and melons, don't fit into this category. They grow on bushes or vines.)

• **Purim (Feast of Lots; Esther's Rescue of Persian Jews)**

A pastry called hamentaschen (Haman's ears), called *oznei Haman* in Israel

Goodies for *shalach manot* (gifts)

• **Pesach (Passover; Exodus from Egypt)**

Bone, chicken neck, or beet (commemorating lamb sacrifice)

Egg (representing Jewish fertility and "hard-boiledness")

Parsley or celery (green vegetable representing spring)

Horseradish root (symbolizing bitterness of slavery)

Charoset (mixture of fruit, nuts, and wine symbolizing mortar for bricks)

Matzo (the bread of affliction; no leavening was used because there was no time to let bread rise in the hasty flight from Egypt)

• **Shavuot (Giving of the Torah on Mt. Sinai)**

Cheese blintzes

Cheesecake

Any dairy food (various explanations are given for this)

• **Tisha B'Av (9th of Av, Destruction of the Temple)**

No food (to commemorate this and other Jewish tragedies)

• **Shabbat (Weekly Day of Rest)**

Challah (recalls showbread in the Temple)

Cholent or *hamim* (a stew that simmers in a crockpot overnight)

M'KOROT

The Forbidden Fruit

In the beginning there was the *adam,* a human being created from the dirt of the ground, *adamah.* In *Midrash Rabbah* the rabbis say that the *adam* was male and female, joined back to back. The "creation of woman" was actually the separation of this being into distinct male and female parts. Eve, the woman, listened to the snake, who told her she would *not* die (as God had said) if she ate from the tree of knowledge of good and evil. The tree was appealing to her eyes and to her intelligence (Genesis 3:6). So she ate its fruit and gave some to her husband also. Because this couple disobeyed the only command that God had given them—not to eat the fruit of just *one* tree, out of many trees—they became mortal and were exiled from the Garden of Eden.

Manna from Heaven

While the Jews were in the wilderness for 40 years, God fed them by sending "manna" down from heaven. It appeared on the ground and bushes every day like the morning dew. It was white and like coriander seed, but it is said that it tasted like whatever food each individual liked best. God instructed the Jewish People to gather the manna every day, and then on Friday to gather a double portion so they would not have to gather it on the Sabbath. This—and flocks of quail sent by God to pacify those who craved meat—sustained the Jews until they entered the Land of Israel.

WRITE

Here are some questions to think about. Use your journal to reflect on them and come up with your own questions as well:

- Imagine the fruit of the Tree of Knowledge. What did it look like, feel like, taste like, smell like? (Hint: Nowhere in the Bible is an "apple" mentioned.)
- What would you have wanted the manna to taste like?
- What do you think made Eve trust the snake?
- What kind of a person was Eve?
- What sort of a friend do you think Eve would be?
- What do you suppose was the Jews' reaction the first time they woke up and saw this strange white stuff everywhere?

Meet
Claudia Roden

Claudia, a Sefardi Jew, was born in Cairo in the 1930s and raised there. She grew up eating many kinds of food: Syrian, Iraqi, Italian, French, Turkish, and Egyptian. She became a cosmopolitan cook and connoisseur of different cuisines. She has written recipe books on Middle Eastern, Italian, and worldwide cuisines. Her most recent book, *The Book of Jewish Food: An Odyssey from Samarkand to New York,* is the story of her life embedded in Jewish travel stories about different foods. That it is also a book of recipes is "icing on the cake." Here is an excerpt:

> The dishes of my aunt Latifa and her cook Nessim were the traditional ones of Jewish Syria. On Thursday night there was always lentil soup, rishta bi ats (homemade tagliatelle—pasta—with brown lentils), or rishta wa calsones (tagliatelle and ravioli stuffed with cheese) and fried fish. On Friday night there was chicken or veal sofrito with little fried potatoes cooked in the sauce under the chicken, kobeba—dumplings—and rice with pine nuts and pistachios. These and dozens more Syrian

dishes are what we get when we visit our families in Los Angeles, Mexico, and Colombia, Paris and Geneva.

THINK ABOUT IT

What are your favorite Jewish foods? What are your favorite non-Jewish foods? Did you have different favorites when you were younger? Have your food tastes changed over time? What does food mean to you? What do you eat for breakfast, lunch, and dinner? Do you eat enough healthy food—whole grains and beans, other proteins (meat, dairy, soy, eggs, nuts), carbohydrates (rice, pasta, potatoes), vegetables, and fruits?

WRITE

Judaism promotes a healthy attitude about eating and food. Food is a symbol of health and freedom. There is food after synagogue services, and when there is a celebration such as a bat mitzvah or a wedding, we have food to celebrate. Some families have traditional Shabbat dinners, which are like weekly Thanksgiving dinners. Certain foods remind us of places, times, people, smells, and textures.

How do you feel about food? Do you like to prepare it, read recipes and food articles, cook it, eat it, or all of these?

What is one of your best food experiences? Do you remember the food your grandparents, other relatives, or friends cooked for you when you were younger?

DO IT

Appreciating Food

One way to appreciate food is to slow down the process of eating. You should always try to make time to sit down and eat; always eating on the run can cause digestive problems. Try the following:

Take a piece of fruit and bring it to the table. Now sit down. Before you start to eat it, take it in your hand and consider the fruit as if you had never seen it before. Maybe this is how Eve felt in the Garden of Eden!

Touch the fruit, feel its texture and its weight. Smell the fruit, inhale the aroma coming from it and think of where this fruit actually originated. Was it from a tree, a field, or a garden patch? Is the fruit local or imported? Imagine what the place it came from looks like.

Look at the fruit and notice its color, texture, shape, and pattern. Now take a bite of the fruit and let it sit on your tongue for a moment as if you have never tasted anything like this before. Listen to the sound of it as you chew.

Continue to eat until you are done. Try to keep your attention on what you are eating, how it feels, smells, looks, sounds, and tastes. Try this with a whole meal sometime. It is a truly mind-altering experience.

Sharing Food

Ma'akhil re'eyvim (feeding the hungry) and *hakhnasat orchim* (inviting guests into one's home) are two more *mitzvot* that have to do with eating in the Jewish community. It has always been a high priority to feed those who are hungry. In earlier times, wedding celebrations were always open to the entire community. That meant everybody. It was not considered "charity"—the word *tzedakah* actually means "justice"—and so hungry, poor, and disabled people did not have to feel degraded.

"All who are hungry, let them come and eat!" We say these words every year at the Passover seder. See for yourself how to do this. Collect canned food from your house and from friends. Arrange to visit a food bank or a homeless shelter with an adult and some friends where you can drop off the cans.

Here are some other activities to fulfill the mitzvah of *ma'akhil re'eyvim:*

- Invite people living in your community who are not part of a family to a Shabbat meal or a regular meal. Family meals are a real treat for someone who always eats alone.
- Find out what local organizations work with the hungry and the homeless and ask if they need any volunteers or help.
- Brainstorm a list with your friends on how you can feed the hungry and help the homeless.
- Donate used clothing to a homeless shelter or volunteer at a soup kitchen, either serving food or keeping company with the people who are eating.
- Bring the issue of malnourished people in the community to the attention of your local rabbi, the president of the congregation, the sisterhood of the synagogue, or the synagogue's social action committee. Ask if you can sit in at the annual board meeting to follow up on your ideas.

What Is *Kashrut*?

Learn

The Torah repeatedly tells us that the purpose of the *mitzvot* is to sanctify our lives in imitation of the Divine. This idea is stated quite clearly in reference to the Jewish dietary laws, known as *kashrut*. After listing the animals that are forbidden for Jews to eat, God says, "For I am *Adonai* your God. You shall sanctify yourselves and be holy, for I am holy" (Leviticus 11:44). The adjective *kasher* means "proper and fit." Like many Yiddish and Hebrew words, *kasher* has entered the English language—as *kosher*—because there is no English word that quite conveys this meaning. Its usage extends beyond food to anything that is right and proper. For example, "My English teacher says it's kosher to leave early for my dentist appointment."

"Keeping kosher" with respect to food is a way of life that your grandparents or great-grandparents may have practiced, even if you do not today. Keeping kosher implies a way of looking at the world, a spiritual discipline and a form of respect for food and eating. The purpose of laws around food is to foster our appreciation for food, to make us aware of what we are putting in our bodies, and to refine our relationship with the world around us.

After the flood, God gave Noah a set of laws that apply to all humanity—for example, not to murder, not to commit robbery, and to set up courts of law. These are called the Noahide Laws and consist of things that we today would regard as self-evident for the ethical functioning of a society. These laws included one dietary restriction: not to eat a limb torn off a live animal. (Evidently people did that!)

For Jews, however, God instituted a great many more dietary restrictions. The laws of *kashrut* have helped to define the Jewish People since biblical times. Keeping kosher means making distinctions and choices. "You are what you eat"—what you take into your body becomes part of you; therefore, take care what you put there. Because the *mitzvot* are designed to make us sanctify life as much as possible, some Jews choose to take on as many of these practices as possible. Others, however, choose to take on just a few. As you learn more about being Jewish, you will decide which practices you wish to adopt. One of those may be keeping kosher. If you don't want to be a vegetarian, it is an excellent way to sanctify meat eating.

The guidelines of *kashrut* fall into three categories: permitted versus forbidden animals, the prohibition of eating blood, and the separation of meat and milk.

Permitted versus forbidden animals. Animals that have split hooves and chew their cud are permitted; those that do not are forbidden. Thus cows, sheep, and goats are permitted; rabbits, pigs, and camels are not. Birds that eat grain and mostly walk on the ground are permitted—such as chickens, turkeys, and ducks. Birds of prey are forbidden. Fish must have fins and scales (e.g., salmon, flounder, carp, tuna). All shellfish is forbidden.

There doesn't seem to be a rational explanation for these laws. Traditional Jews believe there is intrinsic value in following *mitzvot* even when we don't know the reason for them. Early Reform Judaism decided that there were health reasons behind these laws that no longer are a source of concern in modern times and so abandoned them. (Now, however, many Reform Jews are taking a new look at *kashrut.*)

It turns out, interestingly, that the permitted mammals are herbivores and the forbidden ones are carnivores. Shellfish eat garbage from the bottom of the ocean. In ancient times it was considered unhealthy—spiritually as well as physically—to consume animals that kill and eat other animals, because the violent characteristics of such animals would enter the person who ate them (Mishnah, *Chullin* 3:6).

The prohibition of eating blood. Permitted mammals and birds must be slaughtered in a ritual way, called *shechitah,* which involves a swift horizontal cut across the throat with an extremely sharp knife, so as to inflict the least possible amount of pain on the animal. The blood is drained. We are not to eat blood, the Torah tells us, because the soul of an animal is in its blood (Leviticus 17:11). We may consume the flesh of an animal, but not its soul. This applies only to warm-blooded animals. Fish, which are cold-blooded, are not ritually slaughtered, nor is their blood drained.

The separation of meat and milk. The Torah tells us in three different places not to "boil a kid in its mother's milk." A number of different reasons are offered by the rabbis for this law, but again it is a mitzvah for which there is no definite, obvious reason. The prohibition was extended from a goat kid to include *all* mammals, and even birds (which are not milk-producing animals!). Food that is neither meat nor dairy is called *parve.* Vegetables, fruits, grains, fish, eggs, nuts, and oils may be eaten with either dairy or meat meals.

The strictest observance of this law includes having separate dishes, utensils, dishpans, sponges, and so forth for meat meals and dairy meals. However, many Jews who keep separate dishes at home will eat vegetarian and dairy food outside the home, where the utensils are not kosher but the ingredients of the food are.

There are many more details to the laws of *kashrut*. An important thing to remember is these laws are much more about our spiritual and psychological well-being than our physical well-being. Restrictions on the foods we are allowed to consume help to make us appreciative, grateful human beings. Although some people say that eating according to kosher standards is a healthier way to live, the real purpose of *kashrut* is to refine our sensitivities and to make eating a conscious spiritual act.

As noted above, Jews observe different levels of *kashrut*. Some people do not keep kosher at all. Some keep kosher with respect to permitted and forbidden foods but not with respect to mixing meat and milk. Some people avoid serving meat and dairy together but use the same dishes for both types of meals, and some have separate sets of dishes for dairy and meat. Some keep kosher in their homes but not when they go out; others choose to eat only in vegetarian or dairy restaurants. Whatever your decision or ideology about *kashrut*, as you mature you have the opportunity to decide whether *kashrut* is something you want to integrate into your life. If you want to keep kosher, but your parents don't, talk to a rabbi. She or he can help you to work out the difficulties in such a situation.

Points for *Kashrut*

- Keeping kosher is a mitzvah in the Torah.
- Keeping kosher develops sensitivity toward animals, plants, and everything we eat.
- Keeping kosher strengthens Jewish identity and perpetuates an important tradition.
- Keeping kosher adds an element of holiness to the daily act of eating.
- Keeping kosher teaches discipline.
- Keeping kosher is a healthy way to eat (separating meat and cheese, for instance, limits the amount of animal fat you can have in one dish!).

PIRKEI BANOT

Why I Started Keeping Kosher

"It wasn't about dishes, or law, or a way of life. It was only a way of feeling. Without any particular sense of obligation, I felt Jewish, I felt a valuable if occasional differentness, and I wanted to pass that on. I wanted my children to eat stuffed cabbage, then yearn for strudel, not ice cream or flan. It was the least way I could honor the grandmothers." —Elizabeth Ehrlich, *Miriam's Kitchen*

Why My Grandmother Stopped Keeping Kosher

"My mother grew up in a very religious home. The first time her mother broke the dietary laws was in the cattlecar on the way to Auschwitz. Someone had some ham, and people had to eat whatever food was available. People convinced her to have a little." —Karen Erdos

(Note: In a case where saving a life [pikuach nefesh] *means violating a mitzvah, Jewish law states it is more important to save a life.)*

M'KOROT

"Do not cook a young goat in its mother's milk." —Exodus 34:26

"You are to be a holy people to me. You shall not eat the meat of an animal in the field torn by a predator." —Exodus 22:30

"When you carefully observe the dietary laws, and eat slowly and deliberately, without hurriedly swallowing your food, your mind will be purified and the spirit of folly will be subdued." —Rabbi Nachman of Breslov, *Likutei Moharan* 1, 17:3

BLESSINGS

LEARN

Judaism makes time before and after a meal to praise God for the food one is eating. This elevates the physical experience of eating to a spiritual one. By blessing the food before eating, you control your hunger and your body. Making a blessing gives you a chance to reflect on where the food comes from and to be grateful that it has been provided to you. By blessing first and digging in second, you are saying, "Before I respond to the growl in my stomach, I am going to pause and bless the Source of this food."

In traditional Judaism there are blessings to say before eating particular foods. For example, before eating a fruit from a tree, you give thanks to the Creator of "the fruit of the tree." Before eating a vegetable or a ground fruit, you say "the fruit of the earth." When eating bread with a meal, you wash your hands and then say a blessing called *hamotzi*. Bread has its own special blessing because it is seen as the most basic form of food, "the staff of life."

The blessing after the meal is known as *Birkat Hamazon* (Grace after Meals). It reminds us to be thankful for the food we have eaten; for God and the earth, the food's providers; for *Eretz Israel* (the Land of Israel), and for peace in the world. It includes many lively songs. At Jewish summer camps, *Birkat Hamazon* is often transformed into a cheerlike prayer at the end of each meal. A shorter blessing is said if bread is not eaten.

Blessings may be said over food even if you don't keep kosher. However, you should not make a blessing over something blatantly nonkosher (e.g., pork, shellfish, nonkosher cuts of meat, meat and milk combinations).

Do It

Here is a list of blessings for all the different types of foods:

- **Wine, grape juice**

  Barukh Atah Adonai Eloheinu melekh ha'olam borei pri hagafen.

  (Blessed are You, *Adonai,** our God, Ruler of the world, Who creates the fruit of the vine.)

- **Handwashing (before any meal that includes bread)**

  Barukh Atah Adonai Eloheinu melekh ha'olam asher kid'shanu bemitzvotav vetzivanu al netilat yadayim.

  (Blessed are You, *Adonai,* our God, Ruler of the world, Who has sanctified us with the *mitzvot* commanded us about washing hands.)

- **Bread**

  Barukh Atah Adonai Eloheinu melekh ha'olam hamotzi lechem min ha'aretz.

  (Blessed are You, *Adonai,* our God, Ruler of the world, Who brings forth bread from the land.)

- **Cake, cookies, rice, pasta (all grain foods that are not bread)**

  Barukh Atah Adonai Eloheinu melekh ha'olam borei minei m'zonot.

  (Blessed are You, *Adonai,* our God, Ruler of the world, Who creates different kinds of food.)

- **Fruits and vegetables**

  Barukh Atah Adonai Eloheinu melekh ha'olam borei pri ha'etz.

  (Blessed are You, *Adonai,* our God, Ruler of the world, Who creates the fruit of the tree.)

* *Adonai* is often used to stand in for the name of God, Y-H-V-H, which, according to Jewish teachings, may not be pronounced.

*Barukh Atah Adonai Eloheinu melekh ha'olam borei pri
ha'adamah.*

(Blessed are You, *Adonai*, our God, Ruler of the world, Who
creates the fruit of the earth.)

- **Anything else (including meat, dairy, fish, and eggs)**
  *Barukh Atah Adonai Eloheinu melekh ha'olam shehakol n'hiyeh
  bidvaro.*

  (Blessed are You, *Adonai*, our God, Ruler of the world,
  through Whose word all things exist.)

Make a list of your 10 favorite foods. See if you can find the right
blessing for each one. Some people prefer to say a blessing that
does not identify God with masculine words, such as the ones above.
Hebrew itself can't be gender-neutral, because every noun is either
masculine or feminine (as in many European languages). Marcia
Falk, a contemporary Jewish poet, has written an entire prayerbook,
The Book of Blessings, which offers alternative blessings that include
feminine forms. Her version of the last blessing in the list above, for
example, is *Nevarekh et Ein Hechayyim shehakol n'hiyeh bidvarah* (Let us
bless the Source of Life through Whose word all things exist).

EATING DISORDERS

LEARN

How do you recognize an eating disorder? The following are some
of the warning signs. A person with an eating disorder may:

- Gain or lose an excessive amount of weight during a short
  period of time.
- Exhibit significant changes in eating behavior (such as
  excessive dieting, eating alone behind closed doors, refusing

to eat certain foods, or hurrying to the bathroom after meals).

- Be preoccupied with food, weight, counting calories, and cooking for others.
- Have an irregular menstrual cycle.
- Have difficulty eating in public.
- Feel guilty about eating habits and ashamed or tormented by her body.

If you or someone you know has an eating disorder or is displaying some of the symptoms of an eating disorder, then you are doing the mitzvah of *pikuach nefesh* (saving a life) by alerting an adult to the problem and making sure they get professional help.

There are three types of eating disorders: anorexia nervosa, bulimia nervosa, and compulsive overeating.

Anorexia nervosa. Anorexia is essentially starving yourself. This happens to some people who have a distorted body image. They think they are overweight, begin to diet, and never stop. Exercise becomes an obsession, as do counting calories and avoiding real food. We know of a woman who eats and drinks nothing but tiny amounts of pita bread and diet cola. She looks like an inmate in a concentration camp. That may not be simply a coincidence—since she is the child of a survivor of the Holocaust. Anorexia can become a very aggressive disease, even causing death.

Bulimia nervosa. A person with this disorder eats by binging—for example, consuming a gallon of ice cream or an entire cake in one sitting—and then tries to take control by purging—that is, inducing vomiting, consuming large amounts of laxatives, or overexercising. The binging and purging cause dental, throat, and esophagus problems as well as injury to the kidneys and stomach. Sometimes bulimia can be fatal.

Compulsive overeating. Like bulimia, this involves overeating and feeling out of control, but there is no purging. Instead, the overeater feels shame and disgust and may exhibit signs of depression, including mood changes and fatigue.

Jewish girls may become vulnerable to eating disorders because of a clash between Jewish values and modern cultural values.

The booklet *Litapayach Tikvah—To Nourish Hope* outlines three aspects of being Jewish that may relate to eating disorders. First is the emphasis on food in Jewish life. There is a joke that goes, "Every Jewish holiday can be summed up in the following way: We were persecuted, we overcame the persecution—let's eat!" Second, there is a correlation between high pressure to succeed—often found in American Jewish families—and eating disorders. However, a person who looks very successful to the outside world may have no sense of self-worth inside. The tension between an outward appearance of accomplishment and an inner sense of failure can lead to an eating disorder. Third is that often Jewish girls and women do not look like the typical image of white Anglo-Saxon "beauty": tall, thin, and blond. Ethnic women may develop an eating disorder as a result of trying to achieve this image. A little girl whose mother is constantly dieting may be particularly vulnerable to an eating disorder.

PIRKEI BANOT

"An eating disorder is not about food: it is about being empty on the inside. It is feeling that you have no right to exist. If you are anorexic, you are trying to make yourself disappear; if you are bulimic or a compulsive overeater, you are trying to fill the emptiness." —Rabbi Jennifer Rebecca Marx

"In the world of adolescent girls, thinness—sometimes at whatever cost—evokes profound jealousy. We lust for the perfect body.

We crave control over our lives. Even when we publicly condemn those who 'control' their food intake, many of us privately admire their willpower." —Sarah Shandler, *Ophelia Speaks*

FINAL WORDS

Eating is not a simple act, even though we do it every day, several times a day, from the day we are born. Food is a gift that we are privileged to receive.

Jewish life makes use of food as a symbol at various points during the annual cycle and the life cycle. Food represents a plentiful harvest as well as our liberation from slavery. Food means celebration, whereas the denial of food means penitence and self-examination.

The *mitzvot* of *ma'akhil re'eyvim* and *hakhnasat orchim* demonstrate the Jewish belief that nobody should go hungry; nobody should be without food to eat or a place in which to sleep. Some Jews live on a diet that clearly distinguishes them from other people. Keeping kosher is a way of reminding you to think before you eat and not to take your food for granted. The practices of keeping kosher and making blessings remind us of the preciousness of food every time we eat and drink.

Eating disorders also make use of food and eating as symbols: control or loss of control, low self-esteem, and insecurity. If you or someone you know has an eating disorder, help is available.

Take eating seriously. Be conscious of what you eat, where on earth it came from, and how you are eating it.

Mitzvah:
Shmirat Shabbat (observance of
a day of rest)

4 RESTING

I like to be active,
but I am
really stressed!

Dear JGirl,

When I was in school, I sometimes took a "mental health day." I just needed to relax and chill out from the hectic pace and competition of school. People used to laugh when I would say how stressed out I was, but I remember feeling overwhelmed by the homework, the pressure to excel, and the extracurricular commitments I had made. The concept of Shabbat (the Sabbath) meant very little to me. Saturday was the day we sometimes went to synagogue in the morning and had a family lunch afterward, but the afternoon was always jam-packed.

Not until I came to live in Jerusalem in my early 20s did I see how overprogrammed my life was. In Jerusalem, whether you are observant or not, the city observes Shabbat. No buses run; most restaurants and stores are closed; people spend time with their families and friends. Because Shabbat was present in the very atmosphere, I could not help experiencing it on a new level. I realized that I never took time to reflect on the week or to realize how grateful I was for the many blessings in my life. Shabbat provided me with the space to do this.

The idea of taking one day a week to rest is an old one. Even God needed to rest after creating the world. The message Jews took from that was that we too need to stop. Our bodies need a break from dance practice, hanging out at the mall, and going to and from school, carrying our heavy backpacks. Our minds need a break from homework, listening to music, and writing on the computer. It's time to shut off the TV and radio, and make your own entertainment.

In Jewish tradition Shabbat begins 18 minutes before sundown on Friday and continues through Saturday 42 minutes after sundown—a full 25 hours. People light candles, turn off all their gadgets, and focus on more spiritual activities. On Shabbat there's time to spend with family, good friends, or even just yourself. There's time to read for pleasure, sleep, enjoy delicious food, play with your baby cousins, and pray or meditate.

Rest is one of the most neglected and important activities for human beings, especially those who are still growing. A day of rest or even part of a day of rest can make up for all the exhaustion, emotional and physical, that you go through in a week. It helps you to think more clearly and be more productive when you return to school or work.

Shabbat Shalom! Have a great break!

Ali

PREPARATION FOR SHABBAT

Shabbat is a Jewish way to quiet down and discover your connection to the universe and to something greater than yourself. It is a gift. Ahad Ha'am, a 19th-century Zionist, said, "More than the

Jewish people have kept Shabbat, Shabbat has kept the Jewish people." Shabbat is an experience that unites us, calms us, reminds us of what is important in our lives, and makes us distinctly Jewish.

In his book *The Sabbath*, Abraham Joshua Heschel, a great 20th-century Jewish thinker, recommended that we

> set apart one day a week for freedom … a day for being with ourselves, a day of detachment from the vulgar, of independence [from] external obligations, a day on which we stop worshipping the idols of technical civilization and a day on which we use no money…. Is there any institution that holds out a greater hope for [humanity's] progress than the Sabbath?

Shabbat is a day with guidelines for slowing down and taking time to just *be*. You may want to try following some or all of these guidelines to experience a day of rest in the Jewish tradition. You may just want to read about them and perhaps incorporate some of the suggestions that appeal to you in your daily life. If you've never observed Shabbat, start with one or two items and add more as you feel comfortable doing so.

M'KOROT

"Remember the Sabbath day to keep it holy. Six days shall you labor and do all your work, but the seventh day is the Sabbath of the *Adonai*, your God. You shall not do any work—you, your son or your daughter, your male or female servant, your cattle, or the stranger who is within your settlement. For in six days *Adonai* made the heaven and earth and sea and all that is in them, and rested on the seventh day. Therefore, *Adonai* blessed the seventh day and sanctified it." —Exodus 20:8–11

"What was created after it was already Shabbat? Tranquility, serenity, peace and quiet." —*Genesis Rabbah* 17:7

"'I have a precious gift in my treasure vault,' God told Moses. 'Its name is Shabbat. I intend to give this gift to the Jewish People. Go inform them.'" —Talmud, *Shabbat* 10b

---

"There was a monarch who prepared a special wedding canopy. It was intricately carved and adorned; the only thing missing was the bride. So too the world was created intricately and majestically, but the only thing missing was Shabbat." —*Genesis Rabbah* 10:9

"Shabbat adds a sweetness and a rhythm to the week, and all that is needed to begin observing this day of rest are two white candles, a glass of wine, two loaves of bread and a tasty meal with friends or family." —Bradley Shavit Artson, *It's a Mitzvah*

"A person should rise early on Friday morning in order to prepare all that is necessary for Shabbat. Even if one has a full staff in one's employ, one should make it one's business to prepare something personally in honor of the holy day. Thus Rabbi Chisda would mince the vegetables; Rabbah and Rabbi Yosef would chop wood; Rabbi Zeira would light the fire; Rabbi Nachman would arrange his house, bringing out those items needed for Shabbat and clearing away objects used only on the weekdays. We should all follow the examples of these sages and not say, 'Don't expect me to belittle myself with such menial activities!' On the contrary, it lends one dignity to honor Shabbat by preparing for its arrival." —*Shulchan Arukh, Orach Chaim* 250:1

PIRKEI BANOT

"What I like about being Jewish is that you know when to work and when to rest." —Yaffa Yeshayahu, 33

"The Sabbath began at sundown Friday, just as it was dark, but the preparations began on Thursday morning. The good housewives did the marketing, and worked ahead feverishly and hard. The house had to be immaculate, the *kuchen* (coffee cake) baked, the children in their good clothes, to welcome the Sabbath—the day of rest—and peace and gladness…. There was evening service and then we had supper…. Never was the linen more snowy, never the meal more perfect…. In some of the very Orthodox families a prayer was said over the bread and wine and the candles lighted to welcome the Sabbath, but I never [do] that ceremony in our house." —Jennie Rosenfeld Gerstley, *"Reminiscences"—of Chicago in the 1860s and 1870s*

DO IT

Ten Tips to Prepare for Shabbat

The fourth of the Ten Commandments that the Jewish people received on Mount Sinai was to observe the seventh day of the week (Saturday) as a day of rest, relaxation, and spiritual appreciation. Here are some suggestions for how you can prepare for the sweetness of Shabbat each week:

1. Wear something special.

2. Buy a treat (a chocolate bar or a magazine) and reserve it for Shabbat.

3. Help prepare a meal.

4. Clean your room.

5. Send someone a *Shabbat Shalom* message.

6. Call a grandparent or another relative to wish him or her a good Shabbat.

7. Take a long bath or shower and paint your nails or give yourself a face mask.

8. Share a highlight of the week with a member of your family.

9. Invite a special friend over for Shabbat.

10. Find an interesting or inspiring article to share.

BRINGING SHABBAT INTO YOUR SPACE

One way to add to a mitzvah is *hiddur mitzvah* (beautifying the mitzvah). This doesn't mean you have to spend lots of money, it just means spending more time and care on the mitzvah. For example, many people put flowers in their homes in honor of Shabbat. Some people make their own candles, candlesticks, or kiddush cups. This is beautifying the mitzvah of Shabbat.

MEET
Lady Shabbat

In Jewish tradition, Shabbat is feminine. Maybe that sounds strange, but Shabbat has been personified as a female for centuries. Some other names of Shabbat are: Beloved of the Jewish People, Royal Queen, Mother, and Bride. Shabbat has been compared to all of these women in poetry, song, and prayer. The fact that men have been most of the writers of poetry, song, and prayer may account for the many images of Shabbat as feminine. In Hebrew all nouns are masculine or feminine. Shabbat is a feminine noun, as are *Torah, Jerusalem, Shekhinah* (God's Presence), and *Eretz Israel.* All of these major features of Jewish life have been described as feminine.

Shabbat is a day of celebrating Creation and feeling like royalty by resting from worldly cares. It reminds us once a week that we carry this royal spirit within us all the time, if we can just remember it. *Kol k'vodah bat melekh p'nimah* is a way of bringing the Sabbath Queen into everyday life.

Another way we bring to light the feminine nature of Shabbat is through a glorious song called *"Eishet Chayil."* This song is attributed to King Solomon and is found in the book of Proverbs (31:10). *"Eishet Chayil"* is a traditional song sung on Friday nights by a husband to his wife. In many homes, the children also sing it to their mother. In other homes, *"Eishet Chayil"* is sung to the Shabbat Queen or Bride, which has now "entered" the home. Regardless of a person's intention, *"Eishet Chayil"* is a beautiful poem expressing love, appreciation, and gratitude for the glory of women both in an earthly sense and in a mysterious, spiritual sense. Think of a special woman in your life whom you would like to praise and to whom you would like to show gratitude. Write about your feelings of appreciation for her in a poem or a card.

What does it mean to you that Shabbat has a distinctly feminine character? Does this make you feel more connected to Shabbat in any way? How? Are there other female roles besides Queen and Bride that you see applying to Shabbat?

M'KOROT

Shabbat haMalkah (the Sabbath Queen) and *Shabbat haKallah* (the Sabbath Bride) are two feminine aspects of the day of rest that make Shabbat successful. *Shabbat haMalkah* represents structure and order, and *Shabbat haKallah* represents emotion and passion. Shabbat is described as a bride in *L'kha Dodi* (Come, My Beloved), a prayer composed by Rabbi Shlomo Halevy Alkabetz, who lived in the city of Safed in the 16th century.

L'kha dodi likrat kallah	Come, my beloved, to welcome the bride,
P'nei Shabbat n'kabelah	the Shabbat presence, let us receive her.
Bo'i beshalom ateret baalah	Enter in peace, the husband's crown,
Gam besimchah uv'tzahalah	also in gladness and good cheer,
Tokh emnuei am segulah	amid the faithful of a chosen people.
Bo'i kallah, bo'i kallah	Enter, O Bride! Enter, O Bride!

LEARN

In Judaism, some *mitzvot* have deeper feminine connections. One traditional "women's mitzvah" is to set aside a piece of dough from the *challah* (Sabbath bread), as an imitation of what the priests in the Temple did. Anyone, male or female, who bakes bread for Shabbat should perform this mitzvah. (The piece of dough is usually thrown into the fire.)

Women also traditionally light the Sabbath candles. Some say this is because women are usually the "keepers of the flame" in the home; others say it is because of the feminine nature of Shabbat. In liberal Judaism, either women or men may light the candles, and in traditional Judaism a man lights them if there is no woman in his home to do so.

After lighting the candles and reciting the blessing, we may add our own personal prayers for our families, our loved ones, and special needs. This helps us to focus on the meaning of bringing in Shabbat for the entire household. Here is an example: "As I light

Light a Candle and Relax

At dusk, I kindled four candles
And the Sabbath Queen came to me.
Her countenance shone
And the whole world became
    Sabbath...
The song of the wind—
Is the singing of Sabbath
And the song of my heart
Is the eternal Sabbath.
—from "The Sabbath Song,"
    by Kadya Molodowsky and trans-
    lated by Kathryn Hellerstein

these candles, let the light come inside me and fill me and those around me with the presence of Shabbat."

M'KOROT

This is the blessing over the candles that has been recited since at least the seventh century C.E.

Barukh Atah Adonai Eloheinu melekh ha'olam asher kidshanu bemitzvotav vetzivanu l'hadlik ner shel Shabbat (Blessed are You, *Adonai*, our God, Ruler of the world, Who has sanctified us with the *mitzvot* and commanded us to light the Sabbath lights).

It is customary for an individual to light two candles because there are two commandments relating to Shabbat in the Torah: to remember it (Exodus 20:8) and to observe it (Deuteronomy 5:12). Some people light a candle for each member of the family. When the candles are lit, some people close their eyes, take a deep breath, and wave their hands over the candles in a circular motion, bringing the light inward. After they have said the blessing, they open their eyes, and Shabbat has arrived! Does your family have a special custom for lighting the Shabbat candles?

WRITE

Shabbat is a time for your body, mind, and soul to rest. In anticipation of this time, some people like to create something especially for Shabbat: bake a cake, write a poem or prayer, make something beautiful for the Shabbat table or your home. Write about Shabbat—about recharging yourself, connecting with people around meals, at synagogue services, and on walks. You could read what you write at the table or during an *Oneg Shabbat,* a Friday night celebration.

Imagine lighting the candles for Shabbat. Take a moment to write your own thoughts and prayers to be said at that time, in whatever language you like. Next time you light Shabbat candles, use your own prayers.

MEET
Malkah Shapiro

Malkah was a writer from a Polish family of Hasidic Jews before World War II. In her memoir, *The Rebbe's Daughter,* she describes a world that no longer exists because it was wiped out in the Holocaust. Malkah was born in 1894 in Kozienice, Poland, to Rabbi Yerahmiel Moshe Hapstein and Brachah Tzipporah Gitl Twersky, both members of illustrious Hasidic families. In 1908 she married her cousin and went to live with his family near Warsaw. In 1926 she emigrated to the Land of Israel, where she published stories, poems, and essays in Hebrew-language journals. Her book *Mi'Din le'Rahamim: Sippurim me'Hatzrot ha'Admorim* (From Severity to Mercy: Stories from the Courts of the Hasidic Rebbes) was published in 1969.

Hasidism is a Jewish sect that began in Eastern Europe in the 18th century. It was a reaction to the elitism of mainstream Judaism, in which learning and literacy were prized above all. The Hasids emphasized prayer through ecstatic dancing and singing, whereby even a Jew who was not well-versed in Talmud could connect with God. There were different Hasidic groups, each one led by a charismatic rebbe (rabbi). They tried to live "in the Torah" every moment.

In the following excerpt, Shapiro describes a special Shabbat in her home, which was the center of Hasidic life in the region. The Torah portion for that Shabbat tells of the Crossing of the Reed

Sea. In it, the Children of Israel celebrate and sing the Song of the Sea (Exodus 15). Men and women sit separately for prayer at Malkah Shapiro's home.

> The women gathered for prayer in the dining room. When the cantor reading the Torah began chanting his sinuous trills for the Song at the Sea, the women rose from their benches and in a spirit of exaltation began chanting loudly with him. "Then Miriam the prophetess, Aaron's sister, took a timbrel in her hand, and all the women went out after her in dance with timbrels!" (Exodus 15:20). A cry of victory swept through the room.

Shabbat Musicians

Listening to Jewish musicians who sing about Shabbat can be profoundly uplifting and, on Friday afternoon or early evening, a good way to prepare for the day of rest—whether you are cleaning, cooking, studying a Jewish text, or preparing to read Torah at services. It will really put you in the mood!

Neshama Carlebach, daughter of the great Hasidic singing rabbi, Shlomo Carlebach, is the living legacy of a family that expressed its spirit and love of God through song, a crucial feature of Shabbat. Many of her songs are about faith in God and love for the land of Israel. Neshama has a very powerful voice. Some of her CDs are *Dancing with My Soul, Ani Shelach,* and *Journey.*

Debbie Friedman is one of the most widely known Jewish musicians in the world. With her lyrics and music, she encourages people to bring God into their everyday lives, to be spiritual every minute of the day rather than once a week at synagogue. She has released over twenty different CDs, exploring everything from healing to overlooked women in the Bible to, of course, the celebration of Shabbat.

You may also enjoy listening to the Israeli singer Shuly Natan, and the Israeli-American singer, Noa, whose CD is called *Eye in the Sky.*

EXPERIENCES OF SHABBAT

LEARN

An important Jewish concept is *na'aseh venishma,* which means "we will do and we will hear" (Exodus 24:8), meaning that first we will do what God wants, and then try to understand why later. At Sinai, God wanted to know if the Jewish people would accept the Ten Commandments. They were unsure of what the *mitzvot* meant and how they were to observe them, yet they were attracted to and excited about God, so they took a leap of faith and said, "Sure! We will do these *mitzvot,* and eventually we will understand what they are all about."

The same is true for Shabbat. If you have never observed Shabbat before, it can seem like a daunting task to undertake for 25 hours. But if you allow yourself to experience it just once, you'll understand much better what it is.

Shabbat has many rules that can seem overwhelming at first, so try just one a week and see how it feels. For example, instead of watching TV on Saturday afternoon, read a book, go for a walk, take a nap, or visit a friend or neighbor. See how you feel.

Genesis says that God created the world in six days, then rested on the seventh. With all that hard work, God realized that humanity would have a similar feeling after working, going to school, doing homework, and practicing basketball and a musical instrument all week. That is why God created Shabbat.

The Torah says that Shabbat is a day when you should not do any work (Exodus 20:9–10). How does Jewish tradition define *work?* Many activities that are forbidden on the Sabbath don't seem like work (e.g., writing, listening to music, or talking on the phone). The principal activities involved in building the tabernacle, the temporary sanctuary in the desert, inspired the rabbis to specify 39 prohibitions for Shabbat. These are expanded for modern times. For example, the prohibition of kindling a fire now includes the use of electricity (although this is not strictly observed by all Jews). For modern people, letting go of our dependence on dishwashers, TVs, stereos, computers, and even telephones and automobiles, reminds us that we are not masters of the world. If you've ever been caught in an electrical blackout because of a storm, you know how humbling it can be.

Refraining from work gives us the opportunity to enjoy and appreciate the many blessings in our lives. During the week we are so busy with school, homework, extracurricular activities, and our other daily activities that we barely have a moment to reflect on what we are grateful for. Also, by taking a break from the world of creation (which is what God did on the seventh day), we rejuvenate our creative selves. What work would you refrain from doing?

Below are some ways to celebrate Shabbat. The best way to start is to choose one to which you feel very drawn and do it a few times, then go on to the next one that attracts you.

AT THE SHABBAT TABLE

LEARN

The Shabbat table represents the altar of the Temple (Ezekiel 41:22), and the *challah* represents the Temple showbread (Leviticus 24:5–9). We salt the *challah* as the priests salted sacrifices in the ancient Temple (Leviticus 2:13). After the destruction of the Temple, rabbinic Judaism endowed each Jewish home with attributes of the Temple through the celebration of Shabbat. Having dinner with family and friends is a chance to take time to eat, drink, talk, and sing for as long as you want. There is no rush at a Shabbat meal. There is usually a festive atmosphere to it, as people catch up after a hectic week, discuss opinions about events, and enjoy each other's company.

FAQs about Shabbat

Here's a list of frequently asked questions about Shabbat that appeared in *Every Person's Guide to Shabbat* by Rabbi Ronald Isaacs.

Q: Why do we wave our hands over the candles before saying the blessing?

A: We should enjoy the candles and the light before we bless them.

Q: Why do we make Shabbat special by using kiddush wine?

A: Shabbat is like a bride, who deserves honor and wine, which is a sign of wealth and respect.

Q: Why do we use two *challahs* at the meal?

A: When the Jews were in the desert, God sent them manna to eat. "And it came to pass that on the sixth day they gathered twice as much food" (Exodus 16:22). The two *challahs* represent the two portions of manna.

Q: Why do we sing *"Shalom Aleichem"* on Friday night?

A: According to the Talmud, when a person comes home from synagogue on Friday night, angels come along (Shabbat 119b). The song is to welcome these angels.

Q: Why do we wear fancy clothes on Shabbat?

A: Shabbat is different from all the other days of the week. In order to make it special, we dress in nice or new clothes.

Do It

One suggestion for your Shabbat table is for everyone to share a positive story that happened to him or her during the week. This creates a cheerful atmosphere while giving everyone a chance to speak. Other people can ask questions about the story once the person is finished talking. These contributions can range from something personal to a world event. Not only do they enliven the conversation, they often lead to a lot of laughter!

SYNAGOGUE SERVICES

To some people, Shabbat services seem boring and long. Give them a second chance: Take a look around you and see what kinds of Shabbat services are available to you. If you have a friend who attends a synagogue, go with her. Or take another friend and go "*shul* hopping." See how Shabbat is observed at each synagogue.

Another option may be a service in someone's home led by a *havurah* (a group of friends or like-minded people). The *havurah* movement originated in the 1960s as a result of several university students and professors getting together to lead prayers and Torah discussion themselves on Shabbat.

Synagogue may be overwhelming to people because they are not comfortable with the *siddur*, the prayerbook. One way to gain familiarity with it is to use a Hebrew-English *siddur* and focus on a single prayer. Understand its meaning. Ask questions about the intentions of this prayer. Perhaps during the week you could do some further reading on this particular prayer. It will mean more to you as you continue to say it.

PIRKEI BANOT

Sylvia Boorstein is a meditation teacher and a writer, founder of the Spirit Rock Meditation Center in California. She has written many books on meditation, including *That's Funny, You Don't Look Buddhist: On Being a Faithful Jew and a Passionate Buddhist*. Born and raised in Brooklyn, New York, she grew up in an observant family and became interested in meditation in the late 1970s. Along with many other Jews, she found the spiritual techniques of Buddhism to be very useful in her own quest for God. The mother of four and grandmother of seven, she lives in California with her husband.

Proving that Shabbat and its celebrations can fit into our lives in many ways, here's what Boorstein has to say about her experience of the holy day.

> I met my friend Eleanor when I was in the fifth grade and moved into a new school district, and we went all the way through high school together. When we were in grade school, we spent Shabbat morning together at *shul* with our grandmothers. When we got bored with services, we walked around the block together and talked. I'm not sure what we talked about, but I guess we shared our secrets.
>
> I like time for myself, just sitting and looking out a window, or lying in bed before I go to sleep or before I get up in the morning, to let the loose threads of my mind straighten themselves out. I wouldn't call it thinking, exactly. It's more like musing.
>
> I notice these days that a fair amount of my *shul* time on Shabbat is that kind of musing. I know the liturgy well enough so that my eyes pass over the pages, my mouth says the words, and my body stands and sits at the appropriate times, but my mind often takes walks around the block. It comes back from time to time and notices the bar or bat mitzvah celebrant; learns who has gotten engaged or is about to be married, who is sick and needing prayers; what the interpretation of the Torah portion for that week is; and then it goes for a walk again. That's fine with me. It's a long morning, and I need the walks as much as I did when I was young.
>
> The obvious difference between my walks long ago and my current walks is that now they happen while my body stays in *shul*. The other difference is how the secrets get told. These days, I tell them to myself.

Do It

Shabbat Sleepovers

Plan a sleepover with a few friends. You could have a special service for *Kabbalat Shabbat* (Receiving the Sabbath) at the home where the sleepover is going to be, then a meal together with singing. In the morning you could do some Torah study, perhaps examining the Torah portion of the week or something else of interest. You can arrange for a delicious lunch and perhaps a hike in the afternoon. These are just some suggestions. We welcome you to write us with any other ideas you have.

SEUDAH SHLISHIT

At *Seudah Shlishit,* the third meal, on Shabbat afternoon or early evening (depending on the time of year), the day is beginning to wane. The songs and tunes for this meal are more mellow than the songs for Friday night dinner. The prayers express a longing for Shabbat, which will be over soon. This is a good time to tell stories. The food at *Seudah Shlishit* is usually light: salads, vegetables, fruits, breads, and crackers. Taking the time to eat, sing, and share experiences in the late afternoon of Shabbat is a custom that developed from the idea that eating special food makes Shabbat a day of greater joy. Three meals in one day were a luxury in most Jewish societies at one time.

HAVDALAH

Havdalah is the ritual for the conclusion of Shabbat, to distinguish its sanctity from the everyday workweek. Singing is a must, and the more people who are gathered together, the better. It can be done with or without musical instruments, depending on your level of observance. During *Havdalah* we light a candle of six braids symbolizing the other days of the week we are returning to, now that Shabbat is over. We make a blessing over sweet-smelling spices to represent the "extra soul" that Jewish tradition says we receive on Shabbat. The act of smelling the fragrant spices reminds us that Shabbat is also a "fragrance," which we'll smell again in a week. Finally, we make a blessing over a cup of wine, a ritual act we perform at both the beginning and the end of Shabbat.

Do It

This activity, created by Rebecca E. Kotkin, shows you how to make your own braided *Havdalah* candle.

All you need are a sheet of multicolored beeswax, wicks, and scissors.

Cut the beeswax into strips approximately 8 inches by 2 inches. Cut the wicks into 8-inch pieces. You will need three strips of beeswax and three wicks for each candle.

Put a wick along the edge of the long side of a strip of beeswax so that half an inch of wick extends over the top of the wax. This will be the top of your candle. Fold the wax the long way over the wick so that the wick is "trapped" inside the strip of wax. Tightly roll the wax so that you have a long, thin candle.

Repeat with the remaining two strips of wax and wicks.

Put the bottoms of the three thin candles together and press the wax with your fingertips until it fuses together. (Beeswax becomes more malleable from the heat of your hand.) Carefully braid the candles, using light pressure on the wax to repair the cracks that come as you twist the candles together.

Enjoy using your candle to sanctify Shabbat and to carry a spark of Shabbat with you all week long.

ONE STEP FURTHER

We can also bring the tranquility of Shabbat into our weekday lives
with the following activities:

- Meditating
- Taking a bath
- Reading
- Walking
- Being in nature
- Exercising
- Breathing deeply
- Learning Torah

FINAL WORDS

Whether you observe Shabbat in all its rituals and practices, or in
some modified way that is still relaxing, you are partaking in the
essence of Shabbat. The Torah says to remember and observe
Shabbat. There are two aspects of Shabbat: One is the communal
praying, eating, singing, and Torah study; the other is to refrain
from everyday activities and concerns (e.g., jobs, money). People
who observe Shabbat, in whatever manner, nurture themselves and
allow themselves to feel their connection with God, the Jewish
People, nature, and other human beings. They recognize their
part in the larger universe. In fact, many people have learned from
Judaism the importance of a day of rest for the health of humanity.
To have such a reminder every week is a gift of Jewish tradition.

5 FEELING GOOD ABOUT MY BODY

I feel healthy most
of the time, but sometimes
I don't take care of myself.

Dear JGirl,

You're coming into your own. Your body is changing in ways that mean you are now a woman. In some cultures in Africa, Asia, and the Middle East, for example, it's typical for girls your age to get married and start having babies. Some of your great-great-grandparents who lived in other countries were married at the age of bar and bat mitzvah. You have other choices, however.

During your teen years you will become the person solely responsible for your health. Of course, your parents and other adults in your life will still make sure that you see a doctor when you need to and that you have food, clothes, and shelter, but it's up to you to learn to understand what your body is telling you and to keep it healthy.

71

The food you eat, how you exercise, what you do in your free time, how much sleep you get—all these are important for you to monitor, because ultimately you will become totally responsible for your own health and well-being. Someday you may decide that you want to become responsible for the health and well-being of others as well: your life partner, your children, your clients or patients or customers.

That's the key. Your health doesn't affect only you; it affects all the people around you, because they care about you and can be "infected" by you when you are sick—both by the germs you carry and by the low energy and depressed mood you project. The opposite is true, too. When you feel good in your body, soul, and mind, it's as if you are beaming out sunshine to the world. In this chapter you'll become familiar with some ideas that can help you to stay healthy and whole.

L'Chayyim! To life!

Penina

YOUR HEALTH—PARTNERS IN CREATION

LEARN

Without your body, what are you? Your body is what allows you to be in the world, to go from one place to another, to get energy and nutrition from food in order to refuel, to perceive your environment around you, to experience every emotion and to participate in your own life.

Although many Jews accept scientific ideas about creation, including the Big Bang and evolution, it is also commonly believed that when God created the world, there was logic and order to the creation process. God created humans with the hope of having a sincere partnership. First God created land, plants and trees, and animals; then God immediately gave humans incredible responsibilities, opportunities, and privilege by saying, "Be fruitful and multiply, fill the earth and be in charge of it" (Genesis 1:28). God encouraged us to take advantage of all that the world had to offer, yet in a structured, disciplined, and thoughtful way. God doesn't want us to be merely puppets in this world; we are instructed to be team players, active members striving to live in, partake of, enjoy, and improve this world. We therefore have a concept called *Shutafey l'ma'aseh beresheit,* literally meaning "being partners in creation." We are in partnership with God regarding all creation—animals and plants, oceans and rivers, mountains and plains. A partnership is a cooperative effort. In this case, we are in a cooperative effort with God to keep creation going.

One of your main responsibilities is to take good care of yourself: body, mind, and soul. Then as you grow and change, you will find your niche in the world. You will find a task that you are especially equipped to do and that will contribute to the world, its existence, and its betterment.

It is sometimes hard to remember that we are each a small part of one big whole. It is easy to feel separate from others as you go about your life each day, but in reality you are affected by everything that happens in this world: the weather, the economy, terrorism, war, and the good deeds of others.

M'KOROT

"Be very careful for your lives." —Deuteronomy 4:15

"To save one person is to save an entire world." —*Mishnah Sanhedrin* 4:37

"Blessed are you, *Adonai,* our God, Ruler of the world, Who has formed human beings with wisdom and created in them many

passages and vessels. It is well known that if one of these were opened or one of these were closed, it would be impossible to exist."
—Blessing after using the bathroom

"In the hour when *Adonai*, Blessed be God, created the first human, God took it and let it pass before all the trees in the Garden of Eden and said to it 'See my works, how fine and excellent they are! Now, all that I have created, for you have I created it. Think about this and do not corrupt and desolate My World, for if you corrupt it, there is no one to set it right after you.'"
—*Lamentations Rabbah* 7:28

WRITE

In your journal, consider the following questions:

- How do I treat myself?
- What kinds of things do I put into my body, my mind, my soul? (For example, I put lots of fruit into my body; I put lots of words from my reading into my mind; I take walks in nature to put air and sunshine into my soul.)
- How do I protect myself and take care of myself?
- How do I exercise?
- How do I rest?
- How do I feel about my body, my mind, my soul?

IN THE IMAGE OF GOD

LEARN

We have seen that it is a mitzvah to treat ourselves with honor and respect, just as we would treat other people. Is there something special about our bodies, however? Is there a deeper reason for treating our bodies well than simply staying healthy and alive? Yes, there is. We can learn this from the Book of Genesis, which repeats the phrases "God created" *(bara Elohim)* and "in the image of God" *(betzelem Elohim)*. When a phrase or word is repeated, you can be sure something very important is being said. Remember, the Torah was first told orally. People didn't have written copies to read again and again. One of the best ways to make sure listeners remembered a key part of the story was to repeat it.

What does it mean to be created in the image of God? If God is not limited by a physical being, then how is it possible that we humans are created in God's image, since we, in fact, are very physical? Can the image of God be invisible?

One view of being created in the image of God is that the qualities of God are in each of us. God is said to be the third partner, with the parents, in the conception of a child. God's role in conception is to bestow the child with a soul, and through our souls we reflect God. (Unlike some religions, Judaism makes no claim as to *when* the soul enters the body.)

M'KOROT

> Thus God created human beings in God's own image; in the image of God, God created them; male and female God created them. —Genesis 1:27

Jewish tradition teaches that our bodies belong to God. What does this mean to you? Do you think it's true or not?

Do It

Here are some things you can do to treat your body with honor and respect.

- Eat three nutritious meals a day.
- Listen to your body; if you are tired, go to bed early. Take an afternoon nap if you need it.
- Do a variety of leisure activities—some energetic activities (such as karate or a brisk walk) and some restful activities (such as reading, hanging out with friends, or day-dreaming in a hammock).
- Try to do some kind of physical exercise three times a week. Make sure you have a proper warm-up and cool-down, and wear proper clothing and shoes.
- Avoid alcohol, drugs, and cigarettes. These can damage your health, your school performance, and your relationships with your friends and family. Most are addictive and can cause severe physical and mental health problems that will get worse over time.

MEET

Athletes are people who use all of the physical capabilities of their bodies to compete in sports—against other people, or sometimes even against themselves. Like all of us, athletes decide if they will treat their body with honor and respect. When they do train well and fairly, they often become role models for the rest of us.

Do you know about these Jewish female athletes?

- Lillian Copeland, set six world records in three track and field events
- Julie Heldman, tennis, founder of Virginia Slims Tour
- Deena Kastor, fastest female marathoner in American history
- Helen Hines, three-time winner of New York Marathon and two-time winner of Boston Marathon, wheelchair divisions
- Nicole Freedman, cycling, two-time U.S. National Champion

- Kerri Strug, gymnastics, Olympic Gold Medal winner
- Sasha Cohen, figure skating, Olympic medalist
- Sarah Hughes, figure skating, Olympic medalist

PIRKEI BANOT

"One thing I've learned from my body is it's ok to be different. You don't always have to fit in with the 'norm.' You can make your own norm." —Jodi, 13

"Sometimes this face looks so funny / That I hide it behind a book / Sometimes this face has so much class / That I have to sneak a second look." —Phoebe Snow, "Either or Both"

DO IT

Sometimes it can be helpful to envision something in your mind in order to examine it more closely. Here is an exercise you can try yourself or try on a friend or a group. To begin, sit in a comfortable way. Breathe in and out a few times to settle yourself down. Then imagine the following.

Someone has given you a small wrapped gift. Do not open it yet. What you have just been given is the most precious gift you will ever be given in your life. Now think about what is the most precious gift you have ever received. You will get only one of these in your whole lifetime. It is not tangible; it is not something to eat, and it is not the latest electronic gadget or a shopping spree at your favorite store. It is something that many people take for granted. How will you treat it if it's the most precious thing in your life? What will you do to ensure its well-being?

The "gift" is your health. It is yours to take care of forever.

Discuss

There are different kinds of health: spiritual, emotional, physical, and intellectual. How can you stay healthy in each of these areas? What are things that improve your health or hurt your health in each of these areas?

Write

Think about ways in which you would like to improve your health—mental, physical, and spiritual. Exercise, stress reduction, nutrition, yoga, prayer or meditation, and "down" time to relax or to write in your journal as a way of reflecting on your day are all ways for you to improve your health. What is the state of your health and your body now? Is it different now from what it was when you were younger? How? Take time to write about your reactions to this chapter and about the general state of your health. Just thinking about your health is a start in becoming healthier.

Do It

The 7 Habits of Highly Effective Teens is a book that tackles the obstacles you will face as a teenager in a practical and understandable way. The following list is based on an activity in it entitled "Baby Steps," a collection of ways you can make positive changes in your life.

Body

- Give up a bad habit, such as biting your nails, eating too much candy, or drinking too much soda, for one week, and see how you feel at the end of the week.
- Go to bed a half-hour earlier.

- Do something nice for your body (e.g., have a massage, go for a walk, or take a bath).

Mind

- Subscribe to an educational magazine like *National Geographic; New Moon,* a multicultural magazine for girls; or *JVibe,* a magazine just for Jewish teens.
- Read one part of the newspaper every day; as a responsible adult, it is important for you to be well informed about current events in the world.
- Invite a friend to go to the museum instead of going to the shopping mall.

Soul

- Take a one-on-one outing with a family member to spend some quality time together: catch a ball game, see a movie, or go for ice cream.
- Begin to build a collection of something: Favorite cartoons, stamps, photos, movies, books, music, or great jokes; a hobby is a great way to relax.
- Learn to play a musical instrument or experiment with writing songs.

DRUGS, ALCOHOL, AND JEWS: WHAT'S THE DEAL?

Some people are quick to dismiss the problem of drug and alcohol abuse because they believe "Jews don't have those problems." Although throughout history Jews have had low rates of alcohol abuse compared to other groups, everything has changed in the

21st century. Jews in the United States are as susceptible to becoming addicted to drugs and alcohol as people from any other group.

Your body is changing into the body of a woman. Although each girl's body has a different timetable for change, everyone will eventually mature. During this time you may feel insecure about your body. After all, it's not the body you have had ever since you can remember. It's not the body in all the pictures of you as a baby or little girl in your family photo albums. Your core is undergoing so much change; you may wonder if you are the same person you were a year ago or a few months ago when you were still a "girl." You may wonder if you are normal. This, in turn, may influence you to use harmful substances to make you feel better about yourself.

Peer pressure is another reason you may be tempted to use drugs and alcohol. When you are going through this life-altering experience of becoming a woman, whom can you rely on to understand you except other girls going through the same thing? You tend to trust your friends even more than your parents and teachers. When friends tell you something is cool or okay, you are likely to believe them.

But this time in your life is also when you are developing your own opinions about things and you are learning to listen to your own inner voice. This is a prime moment for you to remember the concept of *Kol k'vodah bat melekh p'nimah* (the true majesty of a royal daughter is inside her). This means that you have the right answers deep inside yourself on how you should react to the temptations or pressures to try drugs and alcohol. You have the most authentic, real answer inside yourself. Although you may be hearing lots of other voices that are encouraging you to smoke marijuana or drink vodka, before you make such choices, tap into your "royal voice" and listen carefully.

DISCUSS

What is so appealing about alcohol and drugs, especially in the early years of adolescence? People use these substances for a variety of reasons:

- To feel grown up
- To fit in and belong
- To relax and feel good
- To take risks and rebel
- To satisfy curiosity

What do you think of these reasons? Can you think of more?

Drugs were not discussed much by the rabbis because their use did not become common until the 20th century. Drug and alcohol abuse affects people worldwide, and Jewish teens are no exception.

Cigarette smoking was not revealed to be an addiction or a health risk until a few decades ago. The Jewish community, like others, has only begun to come to grips with the health hazards of smoking. Many years ago tobacco was actually used for medicinal purposes for people with digestive and eyesight problems. Recently, however, the Surgeon General's office has deemed smoking to be one of the leading causes of many cancers and other related diseases, and a number of rabbis have written official opinions saying that smoking goes against Jewish principles.

When used in moderation, alcohol is a significant part of Jewish ritual. Wine defines many important moments of the Jewish life cycle. It is always present for making *kiddush* (the blessing over the wine) at joyous times: a circumcision, a bar or bat mitzvah, or a wedding. It is also an essential part of the Jewish holidays. The use of wine each week on Shabbat may have spared Jews from drinking to excess, as it has always been part of the weekly routine in moderation. Even drinking to excess has been "legislated" in Judaism—to twice a year, on Purim and Simchat Torah. However, in recent times, as Jews have become part of secular culture, alcohol abuse has become more of a problem.

DISCUSS

- What is drug abuse? At what point do you think drug use becomes abuse?
- What do you think leads people to take drugs?
- How would you handle peer pressure when someone is trying to convince you to take drugs?

FINAL WORDS

We are all in this world and in this life together. We all come into this world naked, and we all go back to the earth when we die. What happens in between is up to us. We can let life slip through our hands, or we can live each moment as if it were the only one.

How will you live your life? Will you think often about how precious it is and savor those moments? Or will you hardly ever notice how you live and what you put into your body? Will you let yourself rest? Will you make the most of your body, stretching its limits of endurance and strength? Will you celebrate the abilities of your mind and work it, allow it to explore and wonder? How about your soul and spirit? Will you take time to develop the unseen parts of yourself?

Your health is up to you in so many ways. We are each born with a body, a mind, and a soul. Like farmers working the land, we must learn the tools to cultivate our health the best we can. In this way we also ensure the health of the earth, our home. All life on earth is connected. We have the chance to take the best things from the world, ingest the best foods, breathe the healthiest air, and behave in the healthiest manner. God continuously invites us to be an active partner in maintaining creation. This partnership not only follows Jewish precepts, it also leaves you feeling energized and vigorous. We have a great responsibility to care for our bodies just as we care for our homes, our forests, the animals around us, and the air we breathe. Becoming a JGirl means becoming partners with God, in whose image we are made, and being an active participant in living the healthiest possible physical, emotional, and spiritual life.

6 LIKING MYSELF

I want to fit in,
but I want to be
true to myself.

Dear JGirl,

Who do you think is the most beautiful person in the world? There's no "right" answer to this question, of course. It all depends on what you think beauty *is. As the old saying goes, "Beauty is in the eyes of the beholder." For some, beauty is a physical, external quality. For others, it is more intangible, an inner quality.*

When do you feel beautiful? Is there someone you know and respect who radiates beauty? I'm not talking about wearing the "right" makeup and the "right" clothes. I'm talking about a person in whose presence you feel *beautiful. Maybe it's your teacher, whose beauty appears when she teaches; your friend, whose beauty appears when she sings; your mother, whose beauty appears when she is comforting somebody; or your cousin, whose beauty appears when she plays basketball. True beauty is rarer than deep snow in Jerusalem; people flock to it the way birds flock to warmer climates—and it is lasting, not transient like youth.*

The media—television, radio, movies, music, magazines, the Internet—all have an investment in making the definition of beauty dependent on your buying things. In this chapter there are many questions and tools to help you challenge popular notions of beauty. To protect yourself from being hypnotized by the "Buy this!" mantra pounding away at your brain whenever you watch or read or listen or go online, it can be helpful to learn critical tools that can keep you from being sucked into this. How can you possibly keep a true sense of yourself and the world when everyone is trying to sell you the newest, best, and most?

Girls and women are especially vulnerable to the belief that if we could only buy the product that would make us look a certain way, we would live happily ever after. That would be fine if life were a fairy tale, where the shoe always fits Cinderella, Little Red Riding Hood escapes the Big Bad Wolf every time, and it only takes a kiss to wake up Sleeping Beauty after a hundred years. However, life is more complicated and intriguing than that. The search for beauty is a lifelong process.

Here's to your success!

Penina

INNER BEAUTY

LEARN

At first Adam and Eve were both naked, "and they felt no shame" (Genesis 2:25). According to author Gila Manolson, they were able to see each other for who they were; that is, body and soul were one and the same, as in the way that small children view each other's nakedness. However, after Adam and Eve ate of the tree of the knowledge of good and evil, "the eyes of them both were opened, and they knew that they were naked" (Genesis 3:7). At this point, they lost the gift of insight and began to see body and soul as two separate parts of one person. Thus, the trait of seeing a person first as they appear on the outside started in the Garden of Eden.

That is why it is so important to cultivate the inner qualities of listening to yourself and being true to yourself, which determine the way others think of you much more powerfully than your appearance does.

The mitzvah of *tzniut* is about "modesty"—in the sexual sense (how we dress and how we carry ourselves) as well as in the sense of humility (not being arrogant and vain and understanding the importance of respecting others). It is based on self-esteem. A lack of self-esteem often makes a person act arrogant or show off.

Remember how the evil queen in *Snow White* used to ask every day: "Mirror, mirror on the wall, who's the fairest of them all?" She had to keep checking because she was so unsure of herself, and she couldn't bear to hear that anyone else might be "fairer" than she was.

Self-esteem is more than how you feel about the way you look. It's how you feel about yourself deep inside where nobody else can see. It's unfortunate but true that today it is often difficult for girls to feel positive about their bodies and their appearances, and this affects how they feel about their inner selves.

Tzniut defines a certain way of being in the world. *Kol k'vodah bat melekh p'nimah,* the phrase you have been seeing throughout this book, captures this way of being. At certain times in Jewish history, this verse has been interpreted to mean that women should stay inside the home. However, today it can be understood in a different way, which is useful in describing the real meaning of *tzniut.* It has to do with being confident in your innermost core and wanting to live from that core. That is the place of your authentic self, the place where you confront your true feelings and cannot hide from them.

It can be very difficult to reach this place when you feel pressure to assume an identity that may mask your real self. For example, the media constantly sends this message: If you want to be beautiful and cool, then you have to look the way we are telling you to look and be the way we are telling you to be in this ad, with this model, in this movie, on this television show. In recent years, "cool" has sometimes come to mean dressing in a sexually provocative way, but there is a belief in Judaism that says this detracts from women's dignity.

To remain true to yourself in spite of the constant pounding of these messages is a monumental task. The reward is that you will feel comfortable inside your own skin, and you will be able to convey this quality to others. It will radiate from you. People will want to be around you and be like you, because they want to feel that deep inner peace as well.

One of the beauties of Judaism is that it applauds uniqueness in the world. The concept that encourages us to do this is called *Ner Hashem Nishmat Adam* (the lamp of God is the soul of a person). We believe that this special lamp is really a person's individuality. This means that latent within each person in the world is a special spark. Wonderfully, the world is filled with people who are all different, who all have their own individual insights, experiences, and dreams to share.

While being different might sometimes make you feel strange and scared, other times it probably makes you feel special and unique. Think about your thumbprint. Its pattern is distinctive to you alone—no one else in the history of the world has ever had the same one. And like our individual thumbprints, each of us has some part of our inner soul that is unique to this world. Your job as you become a JGirl is to find your own uniqueness, and to let it shine.

MEET

Queen Vashti

We read the Book of Esther every Purim. Many JGirls know Queen Esther well and have probably been Queen Esther for a day early in their lives. In fact, the verse *kol k'vodah bat melekh p'nimah* could have been written for Esther. She worked quietly, secretly, and effectively to save the Jewish People. But how many of you have played Queen Vashti, a rebellious woman who was banished from the kingdom for saying no to the king?

M'KOROT

"Now it came to pass in the days of Ahashverosh.... He made a feast for all his princes and his servants. They gave them drinks in vessels of gold, and royal wine in abundance, according to the king's bounty. On the seventh day, when the king's heart was merry with wine, he commanded ... the seven chamberlains who served in the presence of King Ahashverosh to bring Queen Vashti before the king with the royal crown, to show the people and the princes her beauty, for she was fair to look upon. But Queen Vashti refused to come at the king's command by his chamberlains. Therefore, the king was very wrathful, and his anger burned in him." —Esther 1:1–12

WRITE

Use your journal to write down your reactions to this story. How do you relate to Vashti? If you had been Vashti, how would you have handled the king's order? Do you think Jews should celebrate Vashti at Purim? Do you think Vashti and Esther would have been friends?

Write Vashti's version of the story or Esther's version. Imagine you are telling the story to your child. Following is a modern version of the story from Vashti's point of view, written by Penina Adelman. (It has an alternative ending.)

Vashti's Story: A Modern Midrash

A long time ago, before the holiday of Purim was on the Jewish calendar, there was a young girl named Vashti who was a princess in the land of Persia. She had always dreamed of going out to see the world. She thought that eventually she would like to be a wife and mother, but there were other roles she wanted to try first, such as traveler, adventurer, and seeker. From a very young age she felt oppressed by life in the palace. It seemed she had nothing to do except let others wait on her hand and foot. She had thoughts and ideas she wanted to share with others to see what they had to say, but her teacher was the only one who had time for this. Her mother and father, the queen and king, were too busy ruling the land.

One day when she was 17, a servant came to tell her that her father wanted to see her right away. She hurried to the throne room and found her father sitting on his golden throne with a young man standing next to him.

"Vashti, I would like you to meet Prince Ahashverosh. Prince Ahashverosh, this is my beloved daughter, Princess Vashti."

Vashti curtsied gracefully, as she had been taught to do, and looked up at her father with a question on her face. The king said, "Vashti, it is time you had a husband. It is time you went out into the world to rule your own kingdom."

Vashti looked down at her feet and said, "Your Royal Highness, I will not go with this man."

Anger made big red blotches on the king's neck and turned his entire face red and purple. "You will do as I say, my daughter, or you will be banished from my kingdom forever!"

"Father, I don't even know this man. And he doesn't know me. How can you expect me to say yes when there are so many, many things I want to do before I settle down?"

"Vashti," said the king, softening a little, "the Prince has seen you from afar and has heard all about you from me and your mother. He offers to marry you, and the offer is a good one. You will marry him."

Vashti thought of her desire to see the world, and she could feel her heart melting before her father. "All right, Father, I will do as you say. But if it doesn't work out, I shall leave him."

Six months later, it was not working out. Prince Ahashverosh did not want to talk with Vashti; he only wanted to look at her in splendid outfit after splendid outfit. She was as beautiful as a young apple tree on the day it first blooms. She was as lovely as the clear stream that flows beneath the tree. She was as heartfelt as the song of the red-winged blackbird perched on the top branch. Ahashverosh liked her to be at his side when he held court, when he ate, and when he went to bed. Otherwise she was on her own. Vashti was lonely. She often imagined leaving the palace to go out into the world as she had always dreamed of doing.

Finally, after her parents had died and she and Ahashverosh ruled the land, there came a day when the new king was feasting with some men of the court and surrounding lands, and he became very drunk. When one of the men suggested that he introduce them to his beautiful wife and she could entertain them with a belly dance, Vashti was summoned.

"What is it, Your Majesty?" she asked, rather irritated.

"O, Queen, you must come before this feast and let us feast our eyes upon you," said Ahashverosh, slurring his words.

"Sire, I will never do such a thing!"

"You'll do it, or you will be banished from my kingdom forever!" shouted Ahashverosh in a rage—just like Vashti's father.

Without even answering, Vashti ran out of the palace, never to be seen there again.

"You see," she explained many years later to her oldest daughter, "they never bothered to know me inside, to know my heart's desires, my dreams. They enjoyed looking at me, but they did not enjoy knowing me for who I am. That is why I had to flee."

MEET

Gabriela Brimmer (1947–2000)

Gabriela was a Mexican-Jewish woman born to two Holocaust survivors. Born with cerebral palsy, she was unable to speak or move her arms and legs. The only parts she could use to communicate with were her expressive face and her left big toe. She used to type out everything she wanted to say on a typewriter on the floor.

She had a lifelong companion named Florencia Morales, who was her primary caregiver, interpreter, and mentor. With her help Gaby was able to attend a mainstream high school and the University of Mexico and to write her memoir, *Gaby: A True Story*, which was a sensation in Mexico and abroad. With Florencia she adopted a baby girl, whom they named Alma Florencia Brimmer. Gabriela Brimmer died in Mexico at the age of 53. Florencia and Alma still live in Mexico City together.

Gaby's memoir was adapted for Hollywood and made into a 1987 film (also called *Gaby: A True Story*) starring Liv Ullman and directed by Luis Mandoki. It is currently being translated into English by Trudy Balch and Avital Bloch.

The struggles Brimmer faced in being accepted by society as much more than "someone with cerebral palsy" demonstrate how difficult it is for people to see beyond the way a person looks.

DISCUSS

Television shows, advertisements, magazines, movies, music videos, radio shows, and websites bombard you every day with the same message: "Buy this, and you'll be happy! Look like this, and you'll be popular! Act like this, and you'll be successful!"

Of course they don't say this outright; they do research to figure out what is the best way to persuade you to buy their product. When is the last time you bought something or wanted to buy it because you saw your favorite singer on TV wearing it, using it, eating it, or driving it?

You need to be media savvy and know when you are being manipulated to buy something or to behave in a certain way. Is the typical *Cosmo Girl*, *Seventeen*, or *Elle Girl* model a normal female body type? Most women do not reach 5'10" and weigh less than 120 lbs. All those pictures in the magazines beckoning you to "buy these clothes and you'll look just like them" are false advertising. Most of us will never look that way no matter what clothes we wear, what makeup we put on, what music we listen to, what movies we see (and why should we want to? Beauty, remember, is in the eye of the beholder!).

One author holds that many girls divide themselves into "false" and "true" selves:

> With puberty, girls face enormous cultural pressure to split into false selves. The pressure comes from schools, magazines, music, television, advertisements and movies. It comes from peers. It comes from parents, from mothers who also suffered from the emphasis on being thin. Girls can be true to themselves and risk abandonment by their peers or they can reject their true selves and be socially acceptable. Most girls choose to be socially accepted and split into two selves, one that is authentic and one that is culturally scripted. In public they become who they are supposed to be. —Mary Pipher, *Reviving Ophelia*

What if you could see right through a person's clothes to their soul? How do you think it would change your impression of them? Remember Joseph and his coat of many colors? Look at the story in Genesis 37. How much did the way Joseph look affect his life? Was he the person everyone could see on the outside, or was he different inside?

WRITE

Write about your own struggle with "inner" and "outer" selves. Is there a quality that people do not see in you that you would like them to see?

Describe this quality of which only you are aware. Do you know other people with this quality? Is there a way in which you could make it easier for the people you care about to see this quality in you?

If you like, write a poem or a story about this quality.

PIRKEI BANOT

"Got new hat and shoes yesterday and I can see it would take but very little to make me give up my life to style, but I hope that such shall never be the case. I do not intend to give my life for 'a cap and bells' but I wish it were so easy for me to decide what I shall give my life up to." —Bella Weretnikow, 17, April 19, 1896

"Tues., 1 Aug. 1944. I'm awfully scared that everyone who knows me as I always am will discover that I have another side, a finer and better side. I'm afraid they'll laugh at me." —Anne Frank, in her last journal entry; she was 15 years old

---

"Flowers are very pretty, bodies of water are very pretty too. I think Ashanti is beautiful … I don't know her because she's famous and stuff, but she is really pretty. I think to be beautiful you have to show it in your actions, being honest, trustworthy, faithful, loving, understanding—all that I find beautiful." —Laura, 13

"Different people have different ways of being beautiful. Some people may have external beauty and others may have beauty in the way they think or act. It's up to each individual to create their own beauty." —Jesse, 15

BODY IMAGE

Judaism recognizes the pitfalls of low self-esteem. In the Bible, when the scouts were sent to the land of Israel, they came back and said, "We looked like grasshoppers to ourselves, and so we must have looked to them" (Numbers 13:33). If you think you are worthless and weak, others will also perceive you as such. It is very easy to fall into this "grasshopper mentality" during your teens because of the emotional, physical, and intellectual changes that are taking place within you.

You may not realize that you are falling prey to low self-esteem. Your outer appearance may feel awkward and uncomfortable. You forget what it means to be valued for your uniqueness. Excellence comes to mean "most attractive."

Body image has a great deal to do with self-esteem. People with negative body image have a greater likelihood of developing eating disorders and are more likely to suffer from feelings of depression, isolation, low self-esteem, and obsession with weight loss. Let's look at the two sides of the body image coin.

With a negative body image, you are convinced that only other people are attractive and your body size or shape is a sign of personal failure; you feel ashamed, self-conscious, and anxious about your body; and you feel uncomfortable and awkward in your body.

With a positive body image, you have a clear, true perception of your shape—you see the various parts of your body as they really are; you celebrate and appreciate your natural body shape and you understand that a person's physical appearance says very little about their character and value as a person; and you feel comfortable and confident in your body.

WRITE

Use the following questions to get you started as you write in your journal.

- How do you see yourself when you look in the mirror or when you picture yourself in your mind?
- What do you believe about your own appearance? Include your memories, assumptions, and things others have told you about your appearance.
- How do you feel about your body, including your height, shape, and weight?
- How do you sense and control your body as you move?

DO IT

Try to remember 10 things you love about yourself, especially when you don't!

Girl power—What I love about myself:

1. _____

2. _____

3. _____

4. _____

5. _____

6. _____

7. _____

8. _____

9. _____

10. _____

FINAL WORDS

Inner and Outer Selves

Each of us has a side we show to the world and a side we keep to ourselves. Sometimes it takes a special person, a friend, a teacher or, perhaps, an older brother or sister to encourage us to show that hidden side to the world.

As Jews, we have often been labeled "different" by other people because of our beliefs and practices. You may feel this especially in December. Everyone wishes you "Merry Christmas!" or "Happy Holidays!" when you celebrated Chanukah weeks ago. The larger society wavers between accepting our differences and condemning them. Because of this, some Jews have gone to great extremes to "fit in" with the people who are their neighbors. However, such fitting in comes at a cost. You can lose yourself and your unique identity when you try to be just like everyone else.

As you become a bat mitzvah and after, you wrestle with how to integrate the various parts of you: girl and woman, Jew and plain human being, young child and mature adult. In the process of putting these parts together, you will probably feel doubts at times about who you really are. Are you the girl your parents and teachers say you are? Are you the girl your friends say you are? Are you the girl nobody really knows but you?

A fable tells of a boy who could not fit in with the people around him, and people thought he was sick, so a Jew was brought in to "cure" him. This story was told by Rabbi Nachman of Breslov. Rabbi Nachman of Breslov (also spelled *Bratzlav*) lived in eastern Europe from 1772 to 1810. He was the great-grandson of the Baal Shem Tov, the founder of Hasidism. Hasidism is a movement in Judaism that emphasizes dance, song, and prayer as forms of worship and ways to connect to the Creator. In Rabbi Nachman's day, it appealed to many Jews who were not privileged to be Torah scholars, because it taught that there were other ways to reach God besides studying sacred texts. Storytelling was one of those ways. Rabbi Nachman was a master storyteller. Here is the story of the boy.

Once upon a time there was a prince who thought he was a rooster. He wandered around the palace, clucking and crowing and waving his feathers just like a rooster. The king and queen were beside themselves. They needed a proper heir to the kingdom. How could their son ever become king?

So a wise man was summoned. This man used to stay hidden in the woods, where he lived in a humble hut all by himself. But when he heard that the king and queen were desperately looking for someone to help their son, he immediately went to the palace.

Right away, he was shown to the room where the prince stayed. He saw the prince sitting naked under a table, gobbling up crumbs. He asked to be left alone with the prince and sat down under the table with him and immediately took off his clothes. The prince looked at the man in wonder. Nobody had sat with him for such a long time.

The wise man began to talk about the fact that he, too, felt like a rooster where he came from. The prince and the man exchanged stories about being a rooster inside and outside the palace. Gradually, the prince began to trust the man.

One day, the wise man asked a servant to bring some hot soup and freshly baked bread from the palace kitchen. As soon as it came, the man began to eat. "Ah," he said, "this tastes so much better than crumbs! Why don't you try some?"

But the prince hesitated. Then the wise man said, "You know, you can eat this good human food and still be a rooster. Watch how I do it." The prince watched as the wise man ate and ate. His mouth began to water and he decided to try some hot soup. It was really good, and yet he still seemed to be a rooster.

So it went for several months. Gradually, the wise man convinced the prince to eat his food at the table instead of under it. Then he convinced the prince to put on clothes. Finally, the wise man invited the king and queen into the room to see their son's progress.

As soon as the royal couple saw the prince sitting at the table, eating real food, dressed in princely garb, they both kissed and hugged the wise man and their son. They were so happy to have him back. The wise man and the prince winked at each other. They knew they were still roosters underneath!

Mitzvot:
K'doshim tihyu (you shall be holy);
Kol k'vodah bat melekh p'nimah
(the true majesty of a royal
daughter is inside her)

7 BECOMING A WOMAN

I am curious about sexuality, but I am
scared about it, too.

Dear JGirl,

The way you feel about sex and sexuality is unique to you. You'll be interested in it when it's your time to be interested, when your hormones signal to you that your body is embarking on a new adventure. You may look at the rest of the human race in a more intense way, noticing details in people's bodies and in their ways of walking and talking that fascinate you. You may become aware of others looking at you in a more powerful way, too. You may size someone up and be attracted. Before you know it, you may feel ready to give yourself heart, soul, and body to this person to whom you feel drawn like a magnet. Your body seems as if it has a mind of its own, completely separate from your old, reasonable self.

How can this be? At the very beginning of your life, you were born into girlhood and all of its joys and hassles. Now you are being born into womanhood. You are being initiated into some of the great mysteries of life.

Unlike earlier times (for example, in the days of the Bible) when a woman's worth was almost totally dependent on her ability to bear sons, you live in a time when women are valued for many things, and you have years before you have to decide whether you want children.

You may begin to have sexual fantasies and desires now, even though you are not necessarily ready to act on them. It's all part of experiencing your new womanly body, your new role in the community as an adult with the potential for carrying on the existence of the human species. It's a big responsibility, and Judaism has wisdom to give you, especially about honoring the divine spark in yourself. It's also an exciting, pleasurable journey of self-discovery.

Happy and safe adventures!

Penina

GROWING UP INSIDE AND OUTSIDE

LEARN

In Jewish tradition the word *k'dushah* (holiness) implies a separation—of what is sacred from what is everyday, or of milk from meat, for instance. Be mindful of what you are doing, rather than going from one thing to the next without giving it a thought.

Acknowledge how amazing it is that you awaken each day, that each part of your body works the way it is supposed to, that the sun rises again and you can start another day. Jewish tradition provides ways for us to think about what we are going to do and notice how we are feeling. It helps us take time to appreciate the life force that courses through us, the same life force that courses through the universe. This is *k'dushah,* and the mitzvah connected with this value is *K'doshim tihyu* (you shall be holy).

"You shall be holy because I am holy," God says to the Jewish People in Leviticus 19:2. Holiness is an inner quality that each person has, a quality that allows us to connect with something greater than us and greater than our lives here on earth. It is like the awe that we feel upon seeing a rainbow, the ocean, or the earth from an airplane, for example. *K'doshim tihyu* means that you inhabit a sacred space and your body is a sacred space, a holy temple.

Considering the story of Adam and Eve in the Garden of Eden offers an opportunity to explore feelings and attitudes about sex and sexuality in a Jewish context. Do you remember that God did not want Adam and Eve to have the knowledge they could get by doing as the snake suggested and eating from the tree? God said to Adam and Eve, "Of every tree in the garden you may freely eat; but of the tree of the knowledge of good and evil, you shall not eat of it; for on the day that you eat of it, you will surely die" (Genesis 2:16–17).

What was God worried about? Why was this knowledge so dangerous? Could the "dying" that would come about by eating from the tree be something other than a physical death? Could it be, instead, a fundamental change in Adam and Eve that would make them essentially different beings?

Knowledge can do that. A new world opened up to you when you started to talk. People responded to you in a different way. They could know what you wanted or didn't want, rather than having to guess. When you began to read, you could learn about things that were not right in front of you. You gained a key to knowing about all sorts of things—some exciting, some boring, some interesting, some dangerous, some beautiful, and some repulsive.

When Adam and Eve ate the forbidden fruit of knowledge, they began to understand that they were two separate beings who could come together and draw apart. They also understood that they were physically different. "The eyes of both of them were opened, and they knew that they were naked; they sewed fig leaves together and made themselves loincloths" (Genesis 3:7).

When Adam and Eve left the Garden of Eden, where their every need had been provided for, the man had to work hard to make food come out of the ground, and the woman had to work hard to make new life come out of her body. Adam and Eve's independence came at a cost. Your independence will also have negative and positive aspects. Now is a time in your life where your body is changing along with your attitudes and desires. You will never be the same again. You have left the small "garden" of childhood for the larger world of adulthood. Now you'll spend the better part of your life learning the unique ways in which you can give to the world.

Sex preserves every living species, but in Jewish tradition sex also has a greater spiritual meaning. It is one of the things that sustains a marriage and brings two people closer together. The sex drive parallels the spiritual drive that can connect people to a force that is larger than themselves. The Jewish view of sexuality transforms this ordinary act into a sacred one.

In Judaism, sex is supposed to happen within a committed, loving relationship, preferably marriage. Orthodox and Conservative Judaism limit this to mature adults of the opposite sex. Reform and Reconstructionist Judaism accept same-sex relationships that meet the same criteria of maturity, love, and commitment.

Your way of thinking about sex has a great deal to do with self-esteem. If you feel positively about yourself, you will have an easier time making decisions about your sexual activity as you mature. Your level of comfort with your body will also determine how you feel about your sexuality.

Teenage girls are often pressured to have sex before they are ready—by boys and, now, even by society (through mass media). Self-esteem will help you to resist such pressure and wait for emotional and physical maturity before becoming sexually active.

WRITE

Open up your journal and write how you feel about Jewish attitudes toward sex and how you think of your own sexuality. What messages does our society give you about sex, and how do these affect you? Write about any thoughts that have occurred to you so far in reading this chapter.

MEET

Dr. Ruth Westheimer

Dr. Ruth is a psychosexual therapist who was born in Frankfurt, Germany, in 1928. After her parents were murdered in Auschwitz, she moved to Palestine in 1942 at age 16 and fought for Israel's independence as a member of the Haganah (the underground Jewish fighting force that was the precursor of the Israeli Army).

Dr. Ruth advocates sexual intimacy as an important part of human life and asserts that it should take place within the bounds of a loving and committed relationship. She is a columnist, a radio and TV talk show host, and a book author. She has even hosted a show just for teens, called "What's Up, Dr. Ruth?"

Dr. Ruth remains a devoted Zionist, visiting Israel frequently and contributing to charity there.

Judy Blume

Judy is an author of books for children and young adults who dared to tackle some of the most difficult issues facing teens, among them, sexuality.

Born in New Jersey in 1938, Judy graduated from New York University. She began writing for children as a suburban mom, searching for a way to express herself. She sold her first story, "The One in the Middle Is a Green Kangaroo," to a magazine in 1969.

She has since written many books for children, teenagers, and adults, which between them have sold more than 75 million copies. Her work has been translated into more than 20 languages. Judy established the KIDS Fund in 1981 to foster better communication between parents and children, and won the American Library Association's Margaret A. Edwards Award for Lifetime Achievement in 1996.

Judy is often praised for her ability to relate to young people and discuss sensitive subjects openly.

THINK ABOUT IT

The successes of Dr. Ruth and Judy Blume come from their knowledge and understanding ways of conveying it. Do you know someone you can talk to and ask questions about sex, someone who will give you accurate information? It could be your mother, your big sister, another older relative, a friend you trust, your doctor, or your bat mitzvah teacher. It's important to have a female friend who has more life experience than you do, one to whom you feel comfortable talking about sex and the changes going on in your body.

CELEBRATING YOUR PERIOD

Jewish girls around the world have had a variety of coming-of-age rituals marking their first monthly period. In some cultures, the coming-of-age ritual was a wedding! The practice among Jews in Ethiopia used to be to make an arranged marriage for a girl before puberty. The girl would live in her in-laws' house as part of the family, but she and her husband would not share a bed until she began to menstruate. In eastern Europe in the 18th and 19th centuries, boys and girls age 12 and older would get married and live as a couple in one of their parents' homes.

Bat mitzvah is a recognition by the Jewish community that a girl has come of age physically and is therefore ready to be an adult member of that community, spiritually and according to Jewish law. There is no link between the bat mitzvah ceremony and menarche (the onset of menstruation), however. Bat mitzvah celebrations occur at age 12 or 13 regardless of when a girl begins to menstruate. That is why it is so important to take time during preparations for your bat mitzvah to focus on the connection between the physical changes taking place in the body and what they mean for you as a Jewish woman.

At the same time, remember that the physical changes are only an outer sign that certain qualities are growing within you as well— *Kol k'vodah bat melekh p'nimah* (The true majesty of a royal daughter is inside her). You may be changing in your own eyes and in the eyes of the world, but the inner changes are much deeper and represent an even greater shift in your being. Now that you have reached the age of bat mitzvah, your community sees in you the potential for carrying on Jewish tradition and for keeping it alive by bringing it into yourself.

This is similar to the lighting of Shabbat candles, which has more than one layer of meaning. When you light the candles, you bring their light into your home by forming circles with your hands. This is an outer sign that Shabbat has begun. At the same time, you bring the light of Shabbat into yourself—that is, you invite the inspiration and comfort of *Shabbat haMalkah* into your inner world as your female ancestors have done for centuries.

A strong taboo on male contact with menstrual blood exists in traditional Judaism. Many people have mistaken this taboo for a negative opinion about the blood and the female body, but as we noted earlier, such "separation" is a sign of holiness in Judaism. Menstruation is a miracle that signals your capacity to bring life into being. Traditional Judaism uses menstruation as a reason for a woman to have a time for herself, to be with her body alone.

In some cultures a girl's first menstruation is cause for celebration. Shortly after a Navajo girl has her first period, she participates in a ceremony during which, according to Navajo belief, she becomes a mythical character called Changing Woman, daughter of Mother Earth and Father Sky. Changing Woman is responsible for the fertility of the earth and human beings. She becomes the girl's guardian spirit, teaching and advising her from that time on, and the community of women who have witnessed the ceremony provide support, both spiritual and material, to the girl.

Some Jews are creating new rituals and new blessings to emphasize the positive, life-giving associations of menstruation. Goldie Milgram, an author and spiritual leader in New York City, has composed the following ritual.

Welcome to the sisterhood, may your life as a woman be filled with blessing! When your flow ceases, [here's] a little ritual that you can do every month to honor the return of your body cycle, to ensure your well-being, and to welcome the restoration of your energy. [When you're ready,] put a pan out to collect rainwater to add to your bath. Just as you are made of *mayim hayim,* living waters, so it is our custom to immerse in a *mikvah,* a pool of living waters at the end of a cycle of life, which is the egg that has finished its season in your body.

Put in perfumed bubbles or soothing salts, if you'd like. As you rest in the tub, you can review the month gone by. What is it that has lost potential this month, what are you letting go of? What is developing in fascinating ways that you wish to nurture? What blessings and strengths do you hope to draw upon, as a new cycle of days begins? Later, you might write these thoughts in a diary. You can shape your thoughts into a prayer and whisper them—that is a tradition that goes all the way back to Hannah in the Bible.

Your monthly *mikvah* is also an important time to check over your body, which is developing so beautifully every day. It is good to enjoy and marvel at the woman you are becoming. [You may want to write the following *mikvah* blessing on a hand towel using washable fabric paint.] Recite [the *mikvah* blessing] and perhaps experience the tradition of the bath as a womb; slip under the water and emerge reborn, into a new month of living and new season of your life. This month, this *mikvah*, is a celebration of your physical arrival as a woman. Mazel tov!

The blessing for immersion is simple:

B'rukhah at Ya, ha-Sh'khinah, chei ha-olamim, asher kidashtanu b'mitzvotekha v'tzivtanu al ha-t'vilah.

Blessed are you *Shekhinah* [the feminine aspect of God], life of all the worlds, who has made us holy with your mitzvot, and commanded us on immersion.

[Here is another blessing that you may want to recite during this ritual.]

B'shem El Shaddai ekra
Melekh ha-olam
avakesh b'riut
u-sh'leimut b'gufi u-v'ruchi
b'chayei avarekh et Adonai
Rofei kol basar,
u-Mafli la'asot

In the name of El Shaddai [Nurturing One] I call out
Sovereign of Eternity,
I request health
and wholeness in my body and spirit
With my life I will bless God (My Threshold)
Healer of all flesh,
Maker of miracles

Rabbi Elyse Goldstein has adapted the traditional blessing said by men every morning in the synagogue, "Blessed are You, Lord our God, Ruler of the World, who has not made me a woman." This blessing has been offensive to many Jewish women, especially in recent times. Rabbi Goldstein's revised version allows us to affirm our creation as women at the moment we get our period once again: *Barukh Atah Adonai Eloheinu melekh ha' olam she'asani ishah.* Blessed are you, *Adonai* our God, Ruler of the World, who has made me a woman.

PIRKEI BANOT

"When I was a freshman in college, [I started] wondering why I had always thought of my period as a bad thing. It was an unequivocal sign of my femaleness. So, why wasn't it just a sign of my normalcy? Why was I still trying to covertly detach a pad from my underwear silently enough so that the person in the next stall—another woman with her own period—wouldn't hear? Why did I both dread and impatiently await it?...

"I decided to try to consciously think of my period as a tolerable, maybe even neat, part of my life. For the first few cycles it was a struggle. Whenever I felt a cramp, in particular, it was not so easy to just say, 'Oh, la di da, my body is beautiful. I can feel it working its magic!' But soon the cramps nearly ceased altogether. And when they [do] come on, as immediately as I [can], I [do] something to make myself feel better. Sometimes it is chocolate. Sometimes it is crumpling up into a ball on my bed or some other quiet place. And in my best moments, I will get into a really comfortable yogic relaxation pose....

"I started to see my sour mood in the week approaching my period as a kind of homesickness. I felt waves of relief when it finally came. My period thus became my coming home, my time when I feel the most myself and the most in tune with the world; a space where there is clarity and light and reason to celebrate how … amazing my body is.... [It is] a reminder of the mysteries that lie under my skin, physical and mystical." —Michelle, 20

LEARN

When you have your period, you are healthy. The blood is a monthly reminder that your body is in harmony with life. You are young. In most cases your body now has the ability to become pregnant, something you may want to happen when you are older and emotionally mature enough to be a parent.

Blessed Be God Who Made Me a Woman

Blessed be God, who made me a woman,
Who made me Eve, mother of all the living;
And who made me Sarah, the ruler of her home;
And who made me Rebecca, the educator;
And who made me Rachel, the beloved one;
And who made me Leah, the fruitful one.

Blessed be God, who made me a woman,
Who made me Tamar, the avenger;
And who made me Shifrah and who made me Puah, the rebels;
And who made me Yocheved, the mother;
And who made me Miriam, the sister;
And who made me Tzipporah, the wife.

Blessed be God, who made me a woman,
Who made me Devorah, the judge;
And who made me Yael, the fighter;
And who made me Peninah, mother and wife;
And who made me Hannah, the blessed poetess.

Blessed be God, who made me a woman,
And who made me Naomi, strong and determined;
And who made me Ruth, faithful and courageous;
And who made me Hadassah, she is Esther, heroine of the
    Megillah;
And who made me Golda Meir, the brilliant leader.

At least once a day I look into the mirror that is in the room,
And in the mirror that is in the street, and I see "that it is good,"
And recite the blessing with pride:
Blessed be God, who made me a woman.

—Anonymous

Judaism makes many distinctions and separations between special things: Shabbat and the rest of the week, light and dark, holiness and the everyday, the time when menstrual blood is flowing and the time when it is not. In traditional Judaism, a married woman goes to a *mikvah,* a ritual bath, after her period. You may choose to observe this mitzvah if you get married.

DISCUSS

Did you, or will you, do anything special to mark your first period? Penina took her daughter out to lunch a few days after her daughter got her period, then they went to a favorite store to buy red things, like soap and candles. Some mothers and daughters go away for a weekend together. Some fathers give their daughters flowers. Perhaps you, your mother, and your friends could come up with a way to make your first period into a meaningful event.

PIRKEI BANOT

"In the 21st century in the Western world, you hardly have to give a thought to your period—at least, compared to what girls and women had to deal with a century ago. Today there are pads, tampons, sponges, and painkillers to make the whole experience as convenient as possible.

"However, it has also become invisible. I remember feeling a real letdown when the blood finally came. Most of my friends had already gotten their periods. I couldn't wait. But then nothing happened. No celebration, no marking of this life-changing occasion, no acknowledgment that I had just entered the worldwide community of adult women. There was only silence and a disappointing sense of invisibility.

"Many years later, in my 30s, I learned of a Jewish practice that marked menstrual periods as part of a woman's life cycle. It was called 'going to the *mikvah.*' At least there was something to mark my period. But it wasn't the same as if I had gone the very first time I got my period." —Penina Adelman, 48

LOVE AND SEX

Rabbi Rebecca Alpert has written about new ways of looking at relationships, love, and Judaism. She considers the words of the prophet Micah: "God has told you, O humanity, what is good. What does *Adonai* require of you but to do justice, to love kindness, and to walk humbly with your God?" (Micah 6:8). Commenting on this verse, she says, "It makes sense to begin with the individual's relationship with God, expressed through her relationship with herself. It is this relationship that enables her to love others and then to translate that love into acts of justice for all humanity—which is for me the ultimate goal."

DISCUSS

How does love figure into your close relationships? Are love and sex different aspects of the same thing? Do they mean an intimate relationship, or can they be totally separated? The most effective way to show you love someone is to give to him or her—physically, emotionally, intellectually, and spiritually. When you love another person, you want to give to him or her. You also want that person to give back to you, to know you in the deepest way, to validate you, to support you, and even to challenge you.

- What is your definition of love?
- Make a list of people you love. Why do you love each of them?
- Are there different kinds of love?

- Can we be obligated to love someone? *Ve'ahavta l'reyakha kamokha* (love your neighbor as yourself) is one of the most important and basic *mitzvot*. What does this mean to you?
- Do you believe in "love at first sight"?
- How do you show someone that you love him or her?

PIRKEI BANOT

"My first kiss—I remember it like it was yesterday. [It was] the summer of 1998. I was 14. He was 15. I had always had a crush on him; he was the cool guy at camp.... He asked me to the camp dance.... After the dance we had an hour before lights out. He asked me if I wanted to go to his cabin. When we walked in, no one was there. I suddenly got so nervous. I didn't understand what was going on, how I agreed to go to the cabin or what was going to happen. Although on the inside I was freaking out, I kept my cool on the outside. We sat on his bed looking at *Rolling Stone* magazine. I felt like he was moving closer to me. My palms began to sweat!... It was finally going to happen—my first kiss. He leaned towards me and looked me in the face and said, 'Tamara, you are really pretty, and I've had so much fun tonight with you. Can I kiss you good-night?'... I looked at him, smiled, and said 'Yes!' He moved closer, his lips touched mine, and we kissed. Magic! Fireworks! My very first real kiss. It didn't last very long. I was a bit confused at first. But it was nice and sweet, and he was very gentle. We were both a bit uncomfortable afterwards, so he kind of just offered to walk me back to my cabin. When I walked through the door, all the girls wanted to know what happened. Although they were begging me to tell them, I really felt like this was something special that I wanted to keep to myself." —Tamara, 23

"I really don't [believe that] gay and straight girls are ultimately the same ... What's hard as a lesbian teenager, in particular a Jewish lesbian teenager, is not just the dating expectations but the constant sense of having to try to conform. [There is a] feeling of marginality, of having to prove yourself doubly as much as everyone else, of becoming more politically aware earlier, of being silenced ... I know that I learned about boundaries and transgression and facade much younger than most of my friends." —Aviva, 24

SEXUAL SAFETY

Once you recognize how sacred your body is, you respect its needs and desires. Others must respect it, too—that means respecting the boundaries you set. In earlier times (and today, still, in some cultures) women were totally dependent on men for their physical and sexual safety, economic stability, and social status.

MEET
Dinah

The story of Dinah, Jacob's only daughter, illustrates the issue of rape and the position of women in the ancient world.

"Dinah, the daughter of Leah, whom she bore to Jacob, went out to see the daughters of the land. When Shechem, the son of Chamor the Hivite, a prince of the land, saw her, he took her, he lay with her, and he afflicted her" (Genesis 34:1–2). Like many a date rapist, Shechem then claims he is in "love" with her and starts to talk sweetly to her. We can only imagine how terrified Dinah must have been—literally, we must imagine, for Dinah's voice is never heard in the Torah. Her father and brothers do all the talking.

Shechem wants to marry Dinah, so his father, Chamor—whose name means "jackass" in Hebrew!—comes to Jacob to arrange a marriage.

In biblical times a woman was considered "damaged goods" if she was not a virgin when she was married. Thus, this would be the only chance Dinah would probably have to marry. Nevertheless, Jacob and his sons considered rape an "obscenity" (Genesis 34:7; Hebrew *n'valah*). Two of Dinah's brothers, Shimon and Levi, hatch a plot. They agree that Shechem may marry Dinah if all the men of his town, the Hivites, are circumcised. Chamor agrees to this; intermarriage with the Hebrews appeals to him because they are prosperous. However, as the men are recovering from their circumcisions, Shimon and Levi enter their town, slaughter them all, and rescue Dinah, who has been held captive at Chamor's palace.

Jacob is angry at his two sons for their excessive violence. "Shall he treat our sister like a whore?" they reply indignantly.

DISCUSS

- What do you think of the revenge taken by Dinah's brothers? If they had killed only the rapist and not all the men, would their action have been justified?
- What do you think Dinah was feeling and thinking? What would you have wanted to happen if you were she?
- What would you say to someone who claimed that Dinah brought the rape on herself (as rape victims are so often accused of doing)? Does any woman or girl ever cause her own rape?
- What do you think motivated Shechem's post-rape feelings of "love"? Why do you suppose his father's name is Jackass?

LEARN

Now that you have met Dinah, let's discuss two Jewish concepts that can serve as a guide to taking control of your life before you get into a situation like hers.

One is *kavod habriot* (honoring all creatures). Just as all creatures in this world are worthy of honor and respect, you too are worthy. Dinah was worthy, too. Fortunately, in our own time (at least in the Western world), a girl's honor and worth no longer depend on whether she is a virgin. Girls' reputations are still much more vulnerable than boys', however. And the society we live in can often make it even more difficult for a teenage girl to resist early sexual involvement. Nevertheless, "no" means "no," and boys and men must respect your boundaries.

The other concept is *betzelem Elohim* (in the image of God). According to the Torah, we were all created in God's image, which means we all have a spark of God in us. Keeping this in mind, we are more likely to treat each other with honor, respect, and even a sense of awe. Animals were not created in the image of God. Humans were instructed to behave in a more dignified way than animals do. This charges us with the responsibility to move beyond the physical and to look at each person with respect. We should be mindful to relate to humans as more than sexual, physical beings.

If you feel uncomfortable with the way another person is treating you and your body, it's important for you to speak up. Find an adult you can trust and tell her what is happening. Also, if someone you know is uncomfortable with the way another person is treating her or him, help this person to speak up. Sexual coercion is a criminal act. However, even more subtle behaviors are reason enough to tell an adult. These include: touching inappropriately, pinching, cornering, writing sexual graffiti, making sexual jokes, spreading sexual rumors, pulling at someone's clothes or underwear, flashing or "mooning," forcing a kiss on someone, forcing someone to touch her or his private parts.

Pressure from a boyfriend should *never* make you feel guilty about refusing to do something you don't want to do. He may try to persuade you by saying, "If you love me, you'll do it." In the 1950s, mothers would tell their daughters, "If he loves you, he'll wait." That advice is still true.

DISCUSS

Having strong personal boundaries is a lifelong protection from all forms of exploitation. How do you protect yourself? Consider the following:

- Parents and other adults can help you to strengthen your personal boundaries by respecting your privacy and taking seriously your feelings and perceptions.
- Parents and other adults can damage your personal boundaries by turning to you to fill their emotional needs or by violating you physically or sexually.
- Learn to say no. It's good to try to make other people happy, but when your desire to please or your fear of disapproval is excessive, you may meet other people's needs at the expense of your own well-being and become an easy target for those who would use you.
- Learn to set limits with other people. You can't be expected to serve another person always at the expense of your own needs. It's not healthy. You may have to enlist others to help you set limits for your own well-being.
- Practice saying no to others who might want to take advantage of you by doing role-plays with friends, teachers, parents.
- When your parents try to make sure you have adequate adult supervision in certain social situations with boys and girls together and try to enforce reasonable curfews, they are trying to lower the risk of dangerous sexual encounters.

PIRKEI BANOT

"When I was little, my parents always told me not to let anyone touch my private parts. I could recite their commandments verbatim. 'You have special parts to your body that no one is allowed to see or touch unless you let them. But don't let too many people see or touch them, because then they won't be special anymore.' Those rules didn't seem too hard to follow, but there was more to them than my parents realized. I didn't either, until one day in eighth grade.

"A friend of mind was going out with this guy. Over the weekend she went to his house, and they kissed. A couple of weeks later she broke up with him. A few days after that, he told everyone in our grade that she was a slut and 'easy.' At first my friend ignored this, but one day when I was walking down the hall with her, two guys screamed out to her, 'Hey, when did you become such a 'ho!' and called her a 'slut.'

"My friend began to cry. I hugged her and told her that they were being immature, but this incident was hard to ignore. It hurt both of us, because it was abusing her sexuality and exploiting it. This falls under the category of sexual harassment.

"The one thing my parents didn't include in their warnings was that words can be counted as sexual harassment, too! If someone has ever made you feel uncomfortable or embarrassed you about your sexuality, recognize immediately that it is wrong. Tell someone: a friend, a parent, or a teacher. Don't think that you are overreacting. It is your sexuality, it is a gift, and it deserves the utmost respect!" —Eliza, 17

FINAL WORDS

Rachel Shnider, 23, felt that there were not enough books for JGirls on coming of age, so she worked for an entire summer at the

Hadassah-Brandeis Institute on creating something new. She collected writings from traditional Jewish sources and from Jewish women and girls, past and present, about menstruation and all the changes girls go through. She says the following:

> I remember when I first began to get sexual feelings. I was so curious about what it would really be like to kiss a boy. My body was changing and developing, and believe it or not I really liked my new womanly curves, for the most part. I was beginning to feel "sexy"—like there were all these new feelings and desires inside me. I wanted someone else to share them with. I wanted someone else to touch and appreciate my body, too. I wanted to dance with boys, kiss them! So did my friends—we'd often confide in each other about our crushes and wonder about what the "boy of the moment" would be like as a kisser. This was all a part of growing up and enjoying our growing bodies.
>
> I remember the first time that I really did kiss a boy. It was a little scary. But I felt ready, and I really wanted it to happen. It felt so nice to be connected with another person. I remember really wanting and liking the feeling of his body touching mine—a feeling that continues to be nice with every new kiss.
>
> Our sexuality is healthy and pleasurable as long as we feel in control of our own bodies and comfortable with our decisions. Being safe and up-to-date on information regarding protection from unwanted pregnancy and sexually transmitted diseases is a good way to be more comfortable and confident about your choices. Keep in mind that we do have to respect ourselves as our bodies grow and change. Part of what makes sexuality so special is being able to respect and appreciate someone else's body while that person does the same for you.
>
> It is important to realize that you, as a developing

woman, are allowed to have sexual feelings. We women are allowed to want to be touched, to touch other people, and to touch our own bodies. As girls, we might only hear about boys wanting sex. But I assure you, it's so normal for us to feel the same way! Just like boys, we are starting to experience sexual feelings—we may be attracted to boys, girls, or both. Experimenting in ways that ensure your safety and comfort level is all part of growing up. So, learn about your body—learn what makes you feel good, learn your limits. And always respect yourself.

8 THINKING BEFORE I SPEAK

I need to say what I feel and think, but
I may be hurting people when I do.

Dear JGirl,

When I was in high school, I learned the hard way that name calling can really hurt and harm people. The story I'm about to tell you has stuck with me all these years. I want to share it with you.

It was the ninth grade and all the girls thought the eleventh-grade boys were so cute. The guys liked us, too, because we were new to the school. After a while one guy started hanging out with a friend of mine, who I'll call Amy. Soon he asked her to be his girlfriend. And she became the coolest girl in school, riding around on the weekends with this "older" guy. He took her to parties with other juniors and to hang out with his older friends.

One Monday morning when I got to school, I heard a lot of whis-

pering in the halls. I wasn't sure what happened. But when I got to my locker a friend came up to me and said "Did you hear about Amy? She is such a slut! I can't believe what she did!" I innocently asked, "What did she do?" My friend answered, "She cheated on Alexander with two different guys! He is devastated. He found out and broke up with her and is telling everyone what a slut she is." I was shocked. I thought Amy was a loyal friend and a really good person. I couldn't imagine why she would do something like that to her boyfriend.

When Amy came to school, she soon found that everyone was whispering about her. She walked down the hall when a bunch of eleventh-grade boys yelled out, "Hey guys, look at that slut strutting her stuff."

Amy left school immediately and didn't come back for days. When she returned, it took her weeks to smile again.

The truth soon surfaced. The story that was ruining Amy's life was a lie. Amy had not cheated on her boyfriend. He had pressured her to have sex with him and when she refused, he called her a tease. He fabricated the whole story to embarrass her. In reality, he was trying to intimidate her because he was scared he would get in trouble for being so aggressive. Unfortunately, people believed the guy and just gossiped about Amy.

Amy never got rid of her new nickname—"the snow white slut." She is now very accomplished, married, and starting a family of her own. But still when people mention her, they remember her as "the snow white slut," and she knows it.

It says in the Talmud that embarrassing someone is like murdering them. I never understood that until the situation with Amy happened. Rumors that defame someone's reputation do have the potential to "murder" someone—Amy before the rumors felt like a different girl than Amy after the rumors. Hateful gossip is actually a sign of weakness, because the gossiper does not have the courage to say these words to the person's face.

In this chapter we will see how far the effects of negative speech can go. We'll also see how refraining from spreading rumors, sharing gossip, and engaging in lashon harah *will make us feel a lot healthier. And remember, if you don't have something nice to say about someone, try not saying anything at all.*

Good luck!

Ali

GUARDING YOUR TONGUE

LEARN

Let's talk about ways to watch your speech. The familiar meaning of *shmirat halashon* is "guarding your tongue"—that is, paying attention to everything you say and weighing whether it really needs to be said. Could your words possibly hurt someone's feelings, damage his reputation, diminish her self-esteem?

In Jewish tradition, guarding your tongue means thinking before you speak, refraining from saying anything negative about another, telling the truth, being cautious about what you say, and considering how what you say could affect others. There are books and formulas with the goal of avoiding hurtful, negative kinds of talk, which are called *lashon hara* (literally, "evil speech"). You can use skillful speech when you open your mouth—speech that helps and encourages people, strengthens relationships, and presents useful ideas.

Jewish girls and women have a lot to say. (They always have, even if it wasn't recorded for posterity.) That is why it is so important to watch over your speech, to be mindful of what you say. You have crucial things to say about Judaism and the Jewish People and the world. You have important questions to ask. Yet even in the most insignificant small talk, we must be mindful of how we talk and what we say.

We all talk about other people. After all, we are only human. We also appreciate it when someone says something good about us, something that strengthens and affirms us.

The way you speak has a big impact on the people around you. Often, you don't think much about what you're saying. You just say it. Do you remember the game Telephone (also called Whispering Down the Lane)? Someone whispers a statement to the person next to her. Then she passes on what she has heard to the person next to her, and so on, until the last person in the group says out loud what she heard. Usually the statement has turned into something very different from the way it started out. Telephone is a great example of what happens when you pass on what you heard. It also shows how easy it is to distort and relay false information.

Guarding your speech takes discipline and understanding. You constantly put yourself in the frame of mind of the person you are going to talk about and remind yourself how hurt you would be if others were talking about you. Eliminating negative speech from your life is a challenge well worth undertaking.

It is important to note that reporting abuse, for instance, is not *lashon hara.* Obviously, you must say something negative about the person who is hurting you. *Shmirat halashon* simply means that you talk to someone who can help you rather than engaging in pointless gossip.

Here are some examples of *lashon hara:*

- Derogatory statements, such as "Tanya said the stupidest thing in class today."
- Damaging statements, such as "I heard that Jacqui's parents are getting divorced because her mother cheated on her father" or "I heard that Stacy had stopped coming to dance practice because she is suffering from depression."
- Insulting statements: "Aliza's clothes look like hand-me-downs from her grandmother. How can she stand it?"

- Emphasizing undesirable traits: "Amy is so clumsy that I fear for my life whenever she's around."
- Belittling statements: "That new girl Emily is so smart. You'd think she wouldn't even give Michelle the time of day. I mean, Michelle can hardly get a full sentence out, but they seem to like each other. Weird."
- False statements: "My father's client owns two seats at the sports stadium, and he promised me tickets to any concert I want to go to."

Outright lying and false testimony are forbidden by the ninth commandment. *Lashon hara* includes gossip as well as slander and libel, which means saying or writing something mean and untrue. Not only is it forbidden to speak *lashon hara*, it is forbidden to listen to it. You should walk away or even stop the speaker by saying you don't want to hear it.

WRITE

Can you think of examples of gossip or negative speech that you either said or heard? What made you say it? Did it have an impact on anyone else? What was your reaction when you heard it? Did you eagerly listen? Use your journal to reflect on these times.

Rabbi Israel Meir Kagan, also known as the Chafetz Chaim ("lover of life"), was famous for his ability to "guard his tongue." In the late 19th century he composed several important works that deal with the laws of *lashon hara* and strategies for fulfilling the mitzvah of *shmirat lashon* successfully. One of the methods he uses is to request assistance from God. The following is one of his prayers:

Gracious and merciful God, help me restrain myself from speaking or listening to derogatory, damaging, or hostile speech. I will try not to engage in *lashon hara,* either about individuals or about a group of people. I will strive not to say anything that contains falsehood, insincere flattery, scoffing, or elements of needless dispute, anger, arrogance, oppression, or embarrassment to others. Grant me the strength to say nothing unnecessary, so that all my actions and speech cultivate a love for Your creatures and for You.

What prayer would you write?

LEARN

There is a Jewish folktale that illustrates the consequences of *lashon hara* with humor. It conveys a major point about *lashon hara:* You never know where your words might go (especially now with e-mail; someone you don't even know can access your words and use them in ways you never intended!). In Joan Rothenberg's retelling of this story, *Yettele Feathers,* the person guilty of *lashon hara* is a woman, although the Talmud's version of the story features a man.

Once there was a woman who said awful things about another person. Realizing later how much she hurt this person, she went to her rabbi and asked, "Rabbi, what can I do?"

The rabbi thought a bit and told the woman to bring him a feather pillow. She brought the pillow and the rabbi said, "Now go outside, rip the pillow open, and shake out the feathers."

She did just that. As she was shaking out the feathers, the wind caught them, causing them to fly everywhere.

The woman returned to the rabbi and said, "I did as you told me. Now what?"

The wise man replied, "Now go back outside and pick up all the feathers."

The woman looked startled and said, "How can I? The wind took them! I don't even know where they are now."

The rabbi said, "Exactly. Just like your words. Once they're out, it's impossible to get them back."

M'KOROT

There are four biblical prohibitions that relate to *lashon hara*:

"Do not go talebearing among your people" (Leviticus 19:16). This is the commandment against being a gossip. If you have a problem with someone, you should talk to that person, not about the person to someone else.

"Do not carry false news" (Exodus 23:1). When you lie to others, God ultimately knows the truth. Once you get caught in a lie, people begin to know you as a liar.

"You shall not curse the deaf or place a stumbling block before the blind" (Leviticus 19:14). This emphasizes how cruel it is to do something to someone who is unable to deal with it (for example, a deaf person can't hear the curse; a blind person can't see the stumbling block). This does not refer only to people who have a physical disability; it can also apply to anyone with limitations of any sort: mental, social, academic, or physical. You should be careful about commenting on the limited abilities of others.

"You shall not take revenge or bear a grudge against your people, but you shall love your neighbor as yourself" (Leviticus 19:18). How many times have you been upset with a friend and not been able to confront that person? When the feelings are not released, the anger is buried and turned into a long-term grudge and desire for revenge.

Discuss

What do these statements from the Book of Proverbs (King Solomon's wisdom) mean to you?

"One who goes talebearing reveals secrets, but one who is faithful of spirit conceals the matter." —Proverbs 11:13

"Pleasant words are like dripping honey, sweetness for the soul, and health for the bones." —Proverbs 16:24

"Death and life are in the power of the tongue." —Proverbs 18:21

How to Combat *Lashon Hara*

- When you are speaking about someone to a third party, omit his or her name. It's a start!
- Before you speak, ask yourself if what you are saying is true. If not, close your mouth or else you'll become known as a liar.
- Ask yourself why you feel the need to speak negatively about someone to a third party. Are you angry at him or her? Are you insecure about something? Think about it before you open your mouth and allow the words to jump out.
- Ask yourself, "Are my words going to harm anyone?" and "How would I feel if someone were talking that way about me?"
- Refrain from jokes that insult others. As Jews, we have often been hurt by anti-Semitic humor.
- When others start to gossip, leave the room. (If you have the courage, object to what is being said.) Just because everyone is doing it doesn't mean that you have to join them.
- Stay away from people who constantly engage in *lashon hara*. Bad behavior has a way of rubbing off on others.

Another idea that can help you to stop yourself before you say something nasty about another person is something every Jew says on Yom Kippur. It's called the *Ashamnu* prayer. *Ashamnu* means "we have sinned." Let's look at the sins that the prayer assumes many of us engage in every year.

> We abuse, we betray, we are cruel.
> We destroy, we embitter, we falsify.
> We gossip, we hate, we insult.
> We jeer, we kill, we lie.
> We mock, we neglect, we oppress.
> We pervert, we quarrel, we rebel.
> We steal, we transgress, we are unkind.
> We are violent, we are wicked, we are xenophobic.
> We yield to evil, we are zealous for bad causes.

What's interesting about this list is how many of the "sins" it includes are about talking or speech. How many of them do you think can be related to *lashon hara*? Notice that betraying and gossiping are high up on the list, even before the terrible sin of killing. Jeering, killing, and lying are even on the same line!

When we say the *Ashamnu* prayer each year, we acknowledge that we do these things, and so must always work to steer clear of them. It's great to start working on this now, avoiding these behaviors altogether or being as little involved with them as possible.

Next Yom Kippur, when you are in a synagogue, either as a pre–bat mitzvah or a bat mitzvah, think about how you've done in resisting the temptation to engage in *lashon hara*.

PIRKEI BANOT

"I know a girl who tries so hard not to gossip. Every night before she goes to bed she reads this tiny book of reminders on not to spread gossip. She also always writes in her journal if she is really frustrated with someone or has a secret to share. I asked her once why she was so good at not spreading gossip. She told me that when she was younger, someone spread a terrible lie about her. Ever since then, she vowed to watch what she says!" —Nicole, 14

"Many girls today are mean to each other.... They talk behind each other's backs, tell secrets, exclude, and do many other harsh things. Perhaps girls are jealous.... Many girls in my grade are rich and buy expensive clothing. Every day at school, they look each other up and down to see what they are wearing. Lots of girls feel better about themselves when they don't like what someone else is wearing. Another issue among girls is lack of trust. When your so-called best friend talks about you behind your back, you feel as if you can't trust her anymore. The thing I hate the most is exclusion. I have been in so many situations where I have been excluded by my good friends. Most of my friends gossip, talk about each other behind their backs, exclude, and do other things that would qualify as rude behavior. I think that girls should be supportive and caring. No one is better than anybody else. What is the point of commenting negatively about someone? In many cases, the mean girls are the ones who are popular, but that shouldn't be the case. We should all learn to love each other and be nice to one another." —Ariela, 13

"I had a teacher in the sixth grade who knew how to make me feel good. She had a saying that made me feel like I could take on the world: 'You should be so proud of yourself.' After working almost a month on a nature project, I was very nervous about presenting it to the class. I had done the research and the work, but I had to talk about it in French! At the end of the presentation, everyone applauded, but I still wasn't sure how I was feeling.... After the class when the bell rang, Mrs. Levy put her arm around me and said, 'You should be very proud of yourself.' She was right! It was then that I realized that no matter what anyone else thought, I had worked hard and accomplished something I had never done before. She made sure her approval didn't matter, that I had to feel good about it for myself." —Lisa, 25

THE CONSEQUENCES OF GOSSIP

MEET

Miriam the Prophet

One of the most prominent women in the Torah is Miriam, the sister of Moses and Aaron. Together the three of them led the Jewish People out of Egypt by using the strengths with which each had been blessed by God.

Miriam was a young girl when Pharaoh, the ruler of Egypt, declared that all Jewish boys were to be killed at birth. Many Jewish men thus began divorcing their wives to prevent the births and subsequent deaths of sons. Miriam's father, Amram, grew increasingly fearful and told her mother, Yocheved, that he had to divorce her for this reason.

Miriam approached her father and explained to him that what he was doing was worse than Pharaoh's decree. She said, "*Abba* (father), don't you realize that if you divorce *Ima* (mother) in order to prevent the birth of boys, you are also preventing the birth of girls?" Considering Miriam's words, Amram returned to his wife. Other Jewish men followed his example and returned to their wives as well.

After Moses was born, Miriam had the idea to stand on the bank of the Nile and watch what would become of her baby brother when his mother placed him in a basket in the river to escape Pharaoh's decree. Miriam then cleverly suggested to Pharaoh's daughter, who found the baby and decided to adopt him, that she bring a Hebrew nursemaid for him. Pharaoh's daughter agreed, and Miriam brought her own mother to take care of her own baby!

When the Jews were finally freed from slavery, Miriam led the women in singing and dancing when they reached the other side of the Sea of Reeds. The Midrash says that during the forty years in the wilderness, water was provided to the Jews from a well that traveled with Miriam. This is based on the sequence of events in the Torah: As soon as Miriam dies, the Jews have a serious water shortage (Numbers 20:1–2).

Miriam's every action was not positive, however. A major story about her concerns *lashon hara.*

"Miriam and Aaron spoke against Moses because of the Cushite woman he had married.... 'Has *Adonai* spoken only to Moses? Doesn't *Adonai* also speak to us?' *Adonai* heard it. The man Moses was very humble, more so than all the people on the face of the earth" (Numbers 12:1–3).

Miriam, who initiated the conversation criticizing Moses, is punished by God with a skin disease, *tzara'at* (often mistranslated as "leprosy"). As result, she has to be confined for a week. During this time, the entire camp of the Israelites comes to a grinding halt—testimony to her importance. Only after the week is up can the Jews begin to travel again.

Aaron, the "listener" of the *lashon hara,* is not punished with the disease, only with the horror and fear one has when a loved one is deathly ill. This might be seen as an even greater punishment. Aaron's punishment was passive because his involvement in the *lashon hara* was passive: He listened and did not object.

The Midrash suggests that Miriam was actually speaking out of sympathy for Moses' wife, Zipporah, whom Moses was ignoring because he was always up on Mt. Sinai talking to God! Miriam was saying, in effect, "We're prophets, too, but we don't ignore *our* spouses!"

DISCUSS

- What do you make of this story?
- Do you think it was fair to punish Miriam actively and Aaron passively? Why or why not?

- Try taking Miriam's point of view and imagine how she must have felt during those seven days when she was confined.
- Do you think Miriam thought God was being "unfair"? Have you ever been singled out for a punishment that you thought was unfair? Have you ever seen this happen to someone else?
- Does the fact that Miriam had good intentions—her concern for Zipporah—make a difference? Have you ever bad-mouthed someone out of concern for that person's possible mistreatment of another?

SILENCE

Silence is many-sided. On the one hand, it may incorrectly signify the absence of "worthy" speech—such as the lack of a written record of the Jewish women's talk over the centuries. On the other hand, silence can be a strong force for good. Shimon, the son of Rabban Gamliel, said, "All my life I have been raised among the sages, and I have not found anything better for oneself than silence" (*Pirkei Avot* 1:17).

Silence is a way to get in touch with the innermost parts of one's being. It can be difficult, but silence may sometimes be what your soul needs to thrive. Can you think of times this has been true for you? Can you imagine times it might have been true for others?

FINAL WORDS

"Words should be weighed, not counted" is an old Yiddish expression. This is true when you are speaking to your friends, teachers, and family. It is also true for yourself. Think about the words you use in describing yourself, your looks, your feelings, your dreams, your conflicts. Be good to yourself in choosing words wisely. A well-chosen word is like a jewel fitting right into its setting.

As a Jewish girl living today, you are fortunate to have more and more words available from women of the past. You can learn what your ancestors were doing, thinking, and feeling. You can see how different and how similar you are from them. Most of all, the voices of Jewish women today are ringing out in ways that will be recorded for posterity.

Rabbi Sheila Shulman of the Leo Baeck Institute in London believes that Jewish women and girls are in a prophetic position. Prophets are people who have always told the truth, describing the world as they see it to the best of their abilities. To say that women and girls are in a "prophetic position" means that we have the potential of saying what it is to be Jewish and whole and fully female and human. As a bat mitzvah, you are finding your voice as a Jewish woman and as a member of the human race. May you learn to take responsibility for your words. May you find your deepest, truest voice and speak proudly in the world.

Mitzvot:
Tikkun olam (repairing the world);
Kol Israel areivim zeh lazeh
(all of Israel are responsible for
one another)

GETTING INVOLVED

I want to make the world
a better place, but there
are just too many problems.

Dear JGirl,

When I was growing up in the sixties, many people thought the world needed to change. We were inspired by several tragic events that followed each other in rapid succession: President Kennedy, and later his brother Robert, were assassinated; Rev. Martin Luther King Jr. was assassinated; and in 1970, four students from Kent State University in Ohio who were protesting against U.S. involvement in the Vietnam War were killed by National Guard soldiers sent by President Nixon to quash the demonstration.

Some of us marched on Washington to protest our government's policies. Some of us went to Woodstock to attend the largest, longest, and most peaceful rock concert ever. Some of us went into the Peace Corps to help people in what were then called "underdeveloped nations." Some of us became active in the women's movement, the civil rights movement, the farmworkers' movement, and, later, the gay rights movement, and the rights-of-the-disabled movement. Some of us became doctors, nurses, lawyers, social workers, professors, teachers, construction workers, plumbers, and other professionals.

After Israel won the Six-Day War in 1967, many young Jewish adults from the United States began emigrating to Israel. There was a sense among many young Jews outside Israel that our fates were intertwined with the fate of Israel.

Some of us began to explore our ethnic and religious roots. Some of us went back to the land, looking for a way of life more in touch with nature. Some of us explored different spiritual paths, from East Indian to Native American, trying to make meaning of our lives. Some of us reclaimed Judaism, learning about Jewish values and spiritual practices with which we could make our lives more meaningful.

A core Jewish value is that wherever you are, you should try to improve things, both in the Jewish community and in the larger world. We know the world is full of things that need improving. There is more anti-Semitism now than there has been since World War II. Terrorism is a global threat. Poverty is growing, and environmental pollution continues to threaten our health—and the health of our planet.

Still, sometimes we and the people closest to us need to work first on fixing ourselves. This is another meaning of Kol k'vodah bat melekh p'nimah—*that is, the inner work must go on alongside the outer work. Thoughtfulness about what we need to improve inside ourselves is essential if we want to improve anything outside ourselves. We must keep going from inside to outside and back again to work on the transformation of our whole planet.*

In the United States, a spirit of volunteering for the sake of the community—whether that is your neighborhood, your school, or your temple or synagogue—has been on the rise since September 11, 2001. Throughout the United States and Canada, people are working on food drives for the hungry and for organizations that build houses for people who need them.

As it says in Pirkei Avot *2:21, "It is not your duty to complete the work, but neither are you free to desist from it."*

B'hatzlachah! Best of Luck!

Penina

MAKE A DIFFERENCE

Whether you are Orthodox, Conservative, Reconstructionist, Reform, or secular, *tikkun olam* is accepted as one of the most important obligations for Jews. *Tikkun olam* literally means "repairing the world." As Jews we have an obligation to look for ways to make the world better, to help others in need, and to find even the smallest ways to improve the world's troubles. It is difficult in this materialistic, self-centered Western world to maintain a sense of responsibility for your neighbor, let alone the rest of the world. While *tikkun olam* can mean saving all the whales, the rain forest, and feeding all the starving children in Ethiopia, it also includes the many small acts of kindness you do every day at home.

According to the Bible, God created the world as a place for people to live. With the privilege of living here also comes the responsibility to care for it. In Jewish belief, every action counts, and every individual has the ability to change the world. As partners with God in this world, it is a Jew's mission to fix things on earth that have been broken. The Talmud (*Sanhedrin* 27b) says, *Kol Israel areivim zeh lazeh* (all of Israel are responsible for one another). This means that every Jew must be attentive to every other Jew's needs. It's similar to saying, "Take care of your family first and then the rest of the world," because all Jews are "family." It also means that whatever one Jew does reflects upon all other Jews. Today, when there is a great deal of anti-Semitism, or hatred of Jews, all Jews are accountable for one another's actions.

It is a good habit to be involved in *tikkun olam* projects in both the Jewish world and the larger, secular world. We know this from the saying of Rabbi Hillel in the Talmud: "If I am not for myself, who will be for me? But if I am only for myself, what am I?" (*Pirkei Avot* 1:14).

WRITE

Take a big piece of paper and draw four concentric circles on it with lots of space between each one. Then fill in the circles according to the following:

> Outer circle: World problems
> First inner circle: Your country's problems
> Second inner circle: Jewish People's problems
> Innermost circle: Your personal problems

Now take a look at today's newspaper. Cut out five or six articles about a world crisis: war, starving children, disease, and drought. Take a look at these articles and write down in your journal the problems that they pinpoint.

Which problem, from these articles or from other crises you are aware of in the world, do you wish you could fix? How would you go about fixing that problem? Which problem in your country do you wish you could fix? Which problem of the Jewish People do you wish you could fix? Finally, which problem in yourself do you wish you could fix? Take some time to reflect on this and use your journal to come up with some ways you could do *tikkun olam* for each of the circles.

Discuss

> Once, while Moses ... was tending his father-in-law Jethro's flocks, one of the kids ran away. Moses ran after it until he reached a small, shaded place. There, it came across a pool and began to drink. As Moses approached it, he said, "I did not know you ran away because you were thirsty. You are so exhausted!" He then put it on his shoulders and carried it back. God said, "Since you tend the flocks of human beings with such overwhelming love—by your life, I swear you shall be the shepherd of My own flock, Israel." —*Exodus Rabbah* 2:2

What do you think about this way of choosing a leader for the Jewish People? How would you choose a leader? Compare with the way in which Rebecca was chosen by Eliezer (see chapter 2).

M'KOROT

"One who saves a Jewish life is considered as if one has saved the entire world." —Talmud, *Sanhedrin* 37a

Hillel said, "If I am not for myself, who will be for me? But if I am only for myself, what am I? And if not now, when?" —*Pirkei Avot* 1:14

"Give to the poor, Jew and non-Jew alike, and thereby bring peace to the world." —Talmud, *Gittin* 61a

"Upon three things the world stands: Torah, divine service, and deeds of lovingkindness." —*Pirkei Avot* 1:2

Putting the World Back Together

Four centuries ago in Safed, a city in Israel that was the center of Jewish mysticism in medieval times, there lived a rabbi named Rabbi Isaac Luria, better known as "the Ari." He would hear about events in the world and wonder how God could allow so many people to suffer and so many injustices to take place. He didn't think that people deserved all the suffering they experienced.

After the Ari thought about this for a long time, he had an insight. He believed that when God finished creating the world, God decided to pour a jar of peaceful, loving light onto it as a finishing touch. As the light was pouring out, the jar suddenly exploded into a million pieces. People suffer today because there are pieces of that light scattered throughout the world, and in order to put an end to the suffering, all of the pieces must be joined back together.

The rabbi was saddened by this thought. How were the Jews supposed to mend a million pieces? It is hard enough putting a jigsaw puzzle together, let alone collecting a million pieces of love and peace. He considered the problem. If people start acting in a peaceful, loving way towards one another, perhaps those pieces of love and peace could reattach themselves.

The Ari then held a town meeting to announce his new findings. The community was receptive to his ideas, and were all inspired to change their behavior. He explained to them that by trying to instill more love, order, and peace in this world, the pieces will re-form. As Jews, one of the most important tasks in life is to find what is broken in this world and repair it. By trying to fix what is broken, saving others from pain and lending a helping hand when in need, we are fulfilling our role as menders of the world.

Do It

Volunteering your time and energy is a crucial part of *tikkun olam.*
Call your city government to find out who is in charge of volunteer services or community service. Contact that person and get a
list. You can also do this with your local synagogue or Jewish
Family Service. Sometimes the local Jewish newspaper lists needs
in the community to be filled by volunteers.

Here are some ideas:

- Visit a seniors' home. The holidays are an especially lonely
  time for many people, especially senior citizens who are confined to a nursing home. Get together a group of your
  friends and go to a nursing home. You have such power to
  bring joy to them by being with them, listening to them,
  singing to them, telling stories, and bringing them holiday
  treats. You can organize this with the local Jewish nursing
  home close to a holiday.

- Beautify a park. Contact the person or department responsible for parks and recreation in your community to find ways
  you can beautify your public spaces. You could plant flowers
  or clean up a local park.

- Assist with Passover preparation. Passover is one of the most
  stressful times all year due to the enormous amount of
  preparation. Perhaps in your community there are families
  who need help with this. Assistance can range from enter-
  taining children to helping an adult cook to scrubbing
  kitchen cabinets.

- Plant trees in Israel. Helping the Land of Israel to grow is a
  way to honor friends and relatives for specific occasions or
  to remember friends and relatives who have passed away.
  Also, consider planting trees in Israel in honor of your
  guests instead of buying elaborate centerpieces of flowers or
  giving out bags of candy at your bat mitzvah party.

- Install a food barrel in your local synagogue or other Jewish communal building. Collect food and distribute to people in need, either through local agencies or individual contacts.
- Make a *tzedakah* box for your home. When it is full, have the entire family decide where the money should go.
- Clothe the needy. Sort through your closet and make a pile of clothing you can donate to a place that accepts used clothing for needy people. By doing this you will be performing the mitzvah of *halbashat arumim* (clothing the naked).
- Adopt a pet with permission from your parents. There are so many animals looking for homes. The Humane Society in your community would be happy to give you a pet for a small adoption fee. Make sure that the animal has received all of its shots and is in healthy condition.
- Choose one day of the week to be your *tikkun olam* day. Make sure you try to "fix the world" in at least two ways, from small things like smiling at the bus driver or saying thanks to your teacher to larger efforts such as helping to make dinner or spending time with a disabled person. Every action makes a difference.

PIRKEI BANOT

"In the past I've done a variety of things. I was part of the leadership team when I was in middle school. We did many projects, such as collecting books to give to people less fortunate, reading books to second graders in the poorer part of Boston, making sandwiches and cupcakes for shelters, and helping animals in need. It made me feel good to do this service, and I know that the people (and animals!) we were helping were very grateful." —Jessie, 15

LEARN

It was young Jewish women in their teens or early 20s, Yiddish-speaking immigrants, who sparked the first general strike of the garment industry.... They were amazing, those tireless, fearless cap-makers, button-makers, waistmakers, corset-makers, and cloakmakers. After long days in brutal working conditions, they organized, preached, rallied, marched.... Singed by exclusion from every side, yet deeply loyal to their ethnicity and to the working class, young women like Clara Lemlich, Paula Newman, Rose Schneiderman and Fannia Cohn defied the male leaders and organized from the grassroots up....They fought with equal fervor for better wages and for education, culture and a more humane way of life....

The housewives were activists, too.... Speechifying to crowds of women from their tenement windows, [they] organized strikes against high-priced kosher butchers and gouging landlords. And it was Lillian Wald, a pioneering social worker at the time, who invented the concept of rent control.

I'm proud to note that Jewish women have made stellar contributions to the modern women's movement, too—Betty Friedan, author of the 1963 groundbreaking work *The Feminine Mystique*, ... Phyllis Chesler, feminist psychologist and writer, Bella Abzug, social activist and politician, and scores of other speakers, organizers, writers and grassroots activists ... we share in the prophetic tradition of idealism and in the outsiders' perspective. —Michele Landsberg, columnist for the *Toronto Star*

MEET

Women Who Are Making a Difference in Jerusalem

- Michal Belzberg, 13, canceled her lavish bat mitzvah party because of all the terrorism that was happening in Israel. She and her family initiated an organization called One Family (www.onefamily.org.il) which helps families who are victims of terrorism.
- Matan Daniel, 17, has taken on the cause of Israeli MIAs (soldiers who are missing in action). She educates people about what they can do to put pressure on the governments and help the families of the MIAs.
- Sarah Miran, 24, started a recycling program.
- Minna Wolf, 32, has initiated an Israeli junior girls' baseball league.
- Barbara Silverman, 73, packages food and presents for Israeli soldiers.

PIRKEI BANOT

"In about a year and half I will serve in the army like every other girl in Israel who reaches the age of 18. In Israel you don't need something specific that will push you to be in *Tzahal*, the Israeli army, because we know, and people keep reminding us, that we have no other choice. I know that I have no other country in the world that I can call home besides Israel, and because of that I will give two years of my life for the country, the Israeli people, and all the Jews around the world, so that they'll have a home in Israel.

"Here in Israel, serving in the army is obvious. We live in a reality in which every day we hear about *Tzahal*'s actions, and we always know that one day it will be us who will need to protect the country. I can say that every child in Israel just knows that.

"And now to you girls around the world...: If you feel as I do that there's no other home like Israel and you feel that there's some kind of a bond between you and your Jewish brothers and sisters in Israel and you want to help them, come and join us in our home and give your best to the country. You can do that by serving in the army, do a *sherut leumi* (national service, like AmeriCorps) or just make *aliyah*.

"I'm a 17-year-old girl from Jerusalem, not religious at all, and basically do stuff just like all of you around the world. Hope to see you all in Israel in the future!" —Matan Daniel, 17

MEET

Queen Esther

The story of Esther is one of many people's favorite parts in the Bible. It's got everything—suspense, mystery, drama, and a beautiful Jewish woman who is courageous and saves her people from the wicked Haman.

Actually, Esther is not unique. In fact, most of the women of the Bible are courageous. But she is special: A whole *megillah*, or scroll, is devoted to her, as is the holiday of Purim.

When Esther was a young girl, she left her family and was taken to a place where she did not know the language and where she was made to live in a harem. Then she was forced to become the queen of a king who spent most of his time giving lavish banquets. Because Esther was so young (maybe your age!) when her story began, she really needed to lean on someone who could guide her. That person was Mordechai, her uncle. Under his guidance and with her new experiences in the royal court, she became mature.

Esther is a heroine for many reasons. She was smart and clever, throwing parties to trick Haman, and even though she's known for her beauty, it is her bravery that we celebrate each year. With a full belief in God, and after a period of intensive concentration through fasting, she decided to risk her life by confronting the king with truth. You know the rest of the story.

Very few people in those ancient days—or now—have the courage to challenge someone who is in a position of power and speak up for what they know is right the way Esther did.

Alicia Silverstone

Alicia, an animal rights activist and a movie star, was born in San Francisco in 1976. She grew up with a passion for performing, acting in her first play when she was three, and modeling by age eight. As an adolescent she had a career based on her beauty, but she maintains a no-nudity policy in all her acting. After appearing in *Crush* (1993) and the Aerosmith video *Cryin'* (1994), she achieved success as a comic actress in *Clueless* (1995). Her success was short-lived as a result of the low ratings of her next two movies, *Batman* (1996) and *Excess Baggage* (1997); she gained weight and became a joke to many actors in Hollywood, but she challenged them all with an undaunted spirit, courage, and Jewish faith.

Alicia is a member of numerous animal rights organizations, including the Ark Trust and Last Chance for Animals. She sends out pro-animal literature in her fan mail and volunteers for animal groups.

Jewish tradition was always important to Alicia's family. Her father encouraged his wife and children to light Shabbat candles and make the blessing over the *challah*. From ages 5 through 13 Alicia studied Judaism three times a week. "I was reared in a traditional Jewish household," she says. "We lit candles Friday night and had seders. I and my brother David went to Hebrew school and had our bar and bat mitzvahs. I have wonderful memories of my bat mitzvah." Despite the thrills and successes in her career, Alicia says she still holds Jewish tradition dear to her. "Sitting in synagogue, singing songs, it's a very close, warm feeling. I feel that religion is in your heart."

Bella Abzug

Bella Abzug, a congresswoman for six years (1970–1976), was born in the Bronx on July 24, 1920.

An outspoken and influential speaker on issues of justice, peace, equal rights, human dignity, and environmental integrity, she was a member of Hashomer Hatzair, a social Zionist organization; she cofounded Women's Strike for Peace (1961), which lobbied against nuclear testing; she was the first congresswoman ever elected on a platform of women's rights; she initiated the Congressional Caucus on Women's Issues; she was a leader at the first UN Decade of Women Conference (1975) and two following conferences; she was named one of the 20 most influential women in the world in a 1977 Gallup Poll mentioned in *US News & World Report*; and she cofounded and led the Women's Environmental and Development Organization in 1990.

After a full life of leadership and fervent activism, she died on March 31, 1998.

FINAL WORDS

Save the whales, save the rain forest, end illiteracy, feed 500,000 starving children—save me!

There are many causes to fight for in this world, and it can be overwhelming to decide which poster to hang up, which company to boycott, whom to support in a presidential election, and where to channel your remaining energy. Sometimes, we are pulled in so many different directions that we don't even remember what matters most.

Tikkun olam seems like a pretty big job. However, *tikkun olam* also includes helping your sibling with homework and making sure a frail older person crosses the road safely.

As a Jewish adult, you are going to be held responsible for your actions. More will be expected of you. One of the responsibilities you will undertake is care and concern for your fellow human beings. When someone is in need of help and you are able to help that person, you extend yourself to do so. You are now going to be responsible for making the world a better place in which to live. That doesn't mean it's up to you to put a stop to nuclear weapons all on your own. It means that you are responsible for looking for opportunities to make someone's day brighter, be of assistance to someone in need, prevent others from getting hurt, and protecting the environment as best you can.

Just as in so many other difficult challenges you might be facing, Judaism has some ideas that can be useful as you consider trying to change the world. The three ideas are balance, balance, and balance.

Balance 1: It is not your responsibility to complete a task of *tikkun olam*—feeding *all* the hungry, housing *all* the homeless—but it is your responsibility to try to do something useful. Instead of demanding the impossible of you, Judaism suggests that you should actively try to help repair the world by doing what is reasonable. That takes you off the hook of too much responsibility

Balance 2: In the whole sea of issues you could get involved in, you should strive for balance between causes that are specific to Jews and Jewish communities and causes that are not specifically Jewish. For example, you could volunteer in your local public library to reshelve books or read to children, and, at the same time, you could volunteer to be a teacher's aide in a Jewish Sunday School. Or you could learn about steps you could take to save the rain forests, while at the same time you could learn about the work of the Jewish National Fund to plant trees in Israel. You'll probably find that the knowledge and experience you gain from working to further one cause will help you with the other.

Balance 3: Find a balance between doing things for yourself and doing things for others. Judaism's teachings do not encourage us to withdraw from the world, to be unhappy, or to intentionally cause ourselves to suffer. Judaism wants you to be happy and be good to yourself. It also wants you to participate actively in this world and pay attention to other people's unhappiness. As it turns out, many times when you do things to make others happy, it makes you happy as well.

Remember, a single act of kindness or improvement can repair the world. *Tikkun olam* is based on action. When your clothes are lying around your room, fold them and put them away. When the milk is gone, buy more. If the garbage bag is full, even though you hate to take it out, do so. *Tikkun olam* is not just about world problems, it can also be about restoring order in your own life. If everyone returned belongings to their owners, kept his or her room tidy, and offered a helping hand when there was a need, the world would be a much better place.

10 BECOMING MYSELF

I am Jewish, but is this how I want to identify myself?

Dear JGirl,

There is a story about a wise Hasidic rabbi named Zusya. As he neared the end of his life, he started fretting and worrying. His students asked him what was wrong. They admired and loved him greatly and were concerned that he seemed to be suffering so much. He told them why he was worrying.

"In the world to come, God will not ask me, 'Why were you not Moses?' God will ask me, 'Why were you not Zusya?'"

You are at a crossroads in your life, gradually leaving the world of childhood and eventually entering the world of adulthood. As you grow up, you are turning more and more into the person you were born to be. It's a good idea to ask yourself Zusya's question from time to time.

Part of who you are becoming includes taking your place as a full member of the Jewish community. There are many, many ways to do this. They are as varied as studying Jewish texts, taking political action on behalf of Jews and other people who need help, attending a Jewish film festival, eating matzah rather than leavened bread during Passover, reading Jewish magazines, visiting Jewish websites, observing Shabbat or attending synagogue. Whether you are a child of two Jewish parents, a child of one Jewish and one non-Jewish parent, or a convert, you will have to decide which aspects of your upbringing you want to bring into your adult life.

In this chapter, you'll hear lots of different girls talking about Jewish identity and what it means to them. You'll also learn about the history and development of the bat mitzvah ceremony. Finally, you'll meet some very accomplished women who have taught and still teach Torah.

Enjoy your journey!
Penina

IDENTIFYING YOURSELF

LEARN

You are the only one who can figure out your identity, Jewish or otherwise. You will find exercises and activities to help, but ultimately the choice and responsibility rests with you.

We are living in a different time from the rest of Jewish history. Up until very recently, if you were born to Jewish parents, you were a Jew. You lived in a Jewish community that most often was situated within walking distance of a synagogue because of the prohibition of riding on Shabbat. You may have spoken the language of the country you lived in when interacting with people outside the community, but you spoke a Jewish language like Yiddish, Ladino, or Judeo-Arabic when interacting with members of your community.

Regardless of our cultural upbringing, we are all descendants of Abraham and Sarah. Although Abraham grew up in a culture where the people believed in many gods and worshipped idols, he rejected that belief system and chose to believe in only one God. As a result, God made a covenant with him, which laid the foundation for Judaism.

Over the centuries Judaism became much more than a belief in one God; it became a way of life. Beginning as nomads, the Israelites eventually moved into cities and towns in the Land of Israel. After the Romans destroyed the Second Temple, the Jewish People scattered all over the world, bringing some customs with them and developing others over the course of time: special ways of preparing food; rituals for celebrating holidays and marking births, weddings, and deaths; stories about their ancestors and about Israel; songs and music; a particular sense of humor; studying the Torah and its commentaries. Everywhere they went, their way of life was affected by the places they lived. Klezmer music plays some of the melodies of eastern Europe and Russia. Jewish food in India incorporated that land's exotic spices. German Jews absorbed the polite, restrained atmosphere of the local churches into their Reform synagogues.

In 21st-century North America, there is a high level of acceptance of being Jewish and a cultural emphasis on individualism. That is how Jewish identity has become a "choice." Many Jews who live in this tolerant atmosphere have become assimilated. We are accepted in places where we used to face discrimination. Ask your grandparents or other people born before World War II if they were allowed to live only in certain neighborhoods in their city or town. Ask if there was a "Jewish quota" in the universities they attended. Find out if there was a ban on Jews in certain companies, hospitals, country clubs, or other social institutions—even hotels.

Today we have blended into so many places within society—at work, at school, in universities, in neighborhoods, in social clubs—that other ethnic groups and even most of the Christian majority in North America consider us equals. Socially, educationally, and financially, we have gone way beyond where many minority communities have been able to go.

Today you can choose your identity, as your immigrant ancestors could not do. If your parents are of two different faiths, you can choose which one you want to adopt, or you can choose not to choose. If you are Reform, you can choose to be Orthodox, or vice versa. It's up to you!

PIRKEI BANOT

Here are the words of several different JGirls about their identity in answer to questions we asked them.

How Do You Identify Yourself?

"I'm a convert, since I was a few weeks old. I was adopted." —Laura, 13

"I'm a 21-year-old female cultural/secular Jew, feminist, New Yorker, Brandeis student pre-med." —Dana, 21

"Thirteen in a few months. American Jew. Loyal friend. Adventurous. Brown eyes and hair. Average height. Nice, kind and helpful." —Talli, 13

"I am Jewish, 12 years old, from Toronto." —Ilana, 12

What Makes You Happy to Be a Jew?

"I enjoyed attending a rally in Washington, DC, and seeing millions of Jews united to support Israel. It felt great!" —Talli, 13

"When we learn about stories in the Torah or *Nevi'im* (Prophets) about the miraculous things Jews have done and God has done for Jews, it makes me feel not really happy but impressed and special, that God would do all these miracles for a small nation that has made a lot of mistakes." —Ilana, 12

"When it nears Christmas, sometimes I have an uncomfortable feeling of being Jewish. It feels weird that on all the surrounding homes there are wreaths except on my door. I feel like I'm being spotted out. I have had the feeling that I wanted to be Christian, but I do like being Jewish. I loved having a bat mitzvah." —Alexa, 14

"The richness of our culture. Also, that I am different from everybody else—namely this country's majority. People are always interested about our traditions." —Rebecca, 15

"I am proud to be part of such a strong, supportive people. Being a Jew classifies me in a category with other Jews, and I like to be able to say to someone, 'Hey, I'm a Jew too!' It's a sense of comfort and automatic acceptance. I like going to *shul* [synagogue] and hanging out with other people who know Hebrew and who understand how hard it is to fast on Yom Kippur. Jews stand up for themselves and get things done. I love being a Jew!" —Ariela, 13

Here is what Margaret, the 12-year-old main character in Judy Blume's *Are You There, God? It's Me, Margaret,* wrote to her teacher about religion.

Dear Mr. Benedict,

I have conducted a yearlong experiment in religion. I have not come to any conclusions about what religion I want to be when I grow up—if I want to be any special religion at all.

I have read three books on this subject. They are: *Modern Judaism, A History of Christianity,* and *Catholicism—Past and Present.* I went to church services at the First Presbyterian Church of Farbrook. I went to the United Methodist Church of Farbrook on Christmas Eve. I attended Temple Israel of New York City on Rosh Hashanah, which is a Jewish holiday. I went to confession at St. Bartholomew Church, but I had to leave the confessional because I didn't know what to say. I have not tried being a Buddhist or a Muslim because I don't know any people of these religions. I have not really enjoyed my religious experiments very much and I don't think I'll make up my mind one way or the other for a long time. I don't think a person can decide to be a certain religion just like that. It's like having to choose your own name. You think about it a long time and then you keep changing your mind.

If I should ever have children I will tell them what religion they are so they can start learning about it at an early age. Twelve is very, very late to learn.

Sincerely,

Margaret Ann Simon

BAT MITZVAH

LEARN

The bat mitzvah ceremony has a very short history, going back only as far as the 20th century. The first known mention of bat mitzvah is in a 19th-century legal code called *Ben Ish Chai* by Rabbi Joseph Chaim ben Elijah al-Hakam. He says that the day a girl becomes a member of the adult community, taking on the mitzvot, is a day of celebration. If her parents can afford it, she should wear a new dress. In this way she can say the *Shehchiyanu* blessing (blessing said over something new) while thinking of her new responsibility to observe the *mitzvot*.

The bat mitzvah ceremony emerged along with the increased education of Jewish girls. Teachers, families, and the girls themselves questioned why boys had a bar mitzvah but there was no equivalent rite of passage for girls. The first girl to ever have a bat mitzvah was Judith Kaplan. On March 18, 1922, she ascended the *bimah* (podium) of her synagogue and read from the Torah. Her father, Rabbi Mordecai Kaplan, the founder of Reconstructionist Judaism, was eager to provide equal opportunities for girls to be active in Jewish life. Judith demonstrated great courage in being the first girl ever to read from the Torah in the United States. Her groundbreaking action opened the door for other denominations of Judaism to make room for girls to have bat mitzvahs. In Reform and Conservative communities, the bat mitzvah became the female counterpart of the bar mitzvah. (Even the traditional age of Jewish adulthood for girls, 12, was changed to 13, to be the same as boys' bar mitzvah age.) The bat mitzvah reads from the Torah or Haftarah and gives a *d'var Torah*, a speech about some aspect of the Torah or Judaism as part of regular synagogue services, just as a bar mitzvah boy does.

Today Orthodox girls also celebrate their bat mitzvahs. A girl may give a *d'var Torah* before the congregation, in the social hall of the synagogue or at home before invited guests. Some Orthodox congregations have a women's prayer group, and the bat mitzvah may chant Torah there, as well as lead the prayers. This practice creates a celebration of the girl's coming of age among women who are accepting her into the larger circle of Jewish women.

As a Jewish girl today, you have many more possibilities and choices open to you regarding how to celebrate your coming of age. This begins with your bat mitzvah, which might include chanting a Torah portion and giving a *d'var Torah,* with a party afterwards. It also might consist of *tikkun olam* activities that you decide to do, both in preparation for your bat mitzvah ceremony and in the years to come.

The ceremony that has developed for boys—chanting Torah, giving a *d'var Torah,* and sometimes leading prayers as well—has become the custom for girls in most Jewish communities today, but the main idea behind bar or bat mitzvah is that now you are an adult and should perform *mitzvot* as part of your everyday life. It could be as simple and private as putting on *tefillin* (prayer phylacteries) for the first time or making a blessing over a piece of food, or as public and intricate as chanting the entire Torah portion in front of the congregation. It could also be working regularly at a soup kitchen or visiting children who are ill in the hospital. One Jewish tradition holds that everyone has a particular mitzvah that is particularly compelling to him or her. Discover what that mitzvah is for you, and then do it as best you can from that time on. This can happen when you have a bat mitzvah ceremony at the traditional age of 12 or 13, or it can happen later. Maybe you didn't have a bat mitzvah ceremony at that age—or maybe you have already had a bat mitzvah celebration but you want to increase your level of Jewish involvement.

The bat mitzvah ceremony can be a public statement of Jewish identity for you and your family, or it can be a more private commitment to become more of a "mitzvah girl." Even if you don't belong to a synagogue or observe Shabbat, even if some of your grandparents are not Jewish, even if your last name was changed at Ellis Island to Smith or Jones, becoming a bat mitzvah means that you are being welcomed into the Jewish community as an adult. This means that you will have more privileges, responsibilities, and opportunities. The bat mitzvah ceremony is just the beginning; an awesome occasion to begin learning, growing, and finding your place as a Jewish woman!

DISCUSS

Here are some questions to discuss with your friends, classmates, family, and people in your Jewish community as well as outside your community.

1. Before you begin, how would you describe your identity? What are the factors that make up your Jewish identity?

2. What do you mean when you say, "I am Jewish"? (If you are curious about how other people have answered this question, a great resource is the book *I Am Jewish,* edited by Ruth and Judea Pearl. It's full of responses to this question from many people—some of them your age!)

3. Who are your Jewish role models?

4. What have been influential Jewish experiences in your life? How have they affected your identity? If you are the child of an interfaith couple, do you consider yourself Jewish, Christian, or something else? How did you come to this answer?

6. In what ways do you feel the same as Jews in the rest of your community, your country, the world?

7. In what ways do you feel different from Jews in your community, your country, the world?

8. Do you think Judaism is a religion? For example, some Jews go to synagogue on Shabbat, keep kosher, and keep a few or many *mitzvot*.

9. Do you think Judaism is a culture? Some Jews like to read books on Jewish history or Jewish poets. Some Jews like to listen to Jewish music—klezmer, Israeli folk tunes, or cantorial music. Some Jews like to cook Jewish food from around the world. Some Jews love bagels and lox on Sunday mornings. Other Jews find connections to Jewish celebrities like Barbra Streisand and Jerry Seinfeld. What does this mean to you?

10. Do you think Judaism is a race? Hitler defined the Jews that way. He declared they were Jewish if one grandparent had been Jewish. All Jews are not the same color, however. There are black Jews from Ethiopia, Asian Jews from China and Japan, dark-skinned Jews from the Middle East, and blond-haired, blue-eyed Polish Jews.

The following poem by Muriel Rukeyser was written in 1944, at the very end of World War II and the Holocaust. How do you think this affected the way she wrote the poem?

Letter to the Front
To be a Jew in the twentieth century
Is to be offered a gift. If you refuse,
Wishing to be invisible, you choose
Death of the spirit, the stone insanity.
Accepting, take full life. Full agonies:
Your evening deep in labyrinthine blood
Of those who resist, fail, and resist; and God
Reduced to a hostage among hostages.

The gift is torment. Not alone the still
Torture, isolation; or torture of the flesh.

That may come also. But the accepting wish,
The whole and fertile spirit as guarantee
For every human freedom, suffering to be free,
Daring to live for the impossible.
—Muriel Rukeyser, "Letter to the Front"

Do It

The best way to live the mitzvah of bat mitzvah is to become a "mitzvah girl." The best way to find your Jewish identity may include talking to other people. Here are some possible projects for you to undertake:

- Make a videotape or audiotape about bat mitzvah. Ask older girls and women what their bat mitzvah experience was like. If they did not have a bat mitzvah ceremony, ask them to talk about a defining moment in their life when they felt that they had crossed the line to become a Jewish woman.

- Ask people from different cultures what is important to them about their culture. What do they like about it? What do they not like about it? What aspects of the culture give them strength and a positive sense of self-esteem? What aspects of the culture are they embarrassed about or not comfortable about sharing in public?

- Ask your parents, grandparents, teachers, or rabbi: What makes you a Jew? What makes you proud to be a Jew?

- Choose an issue in your life that is important to you, such as friendships, including and excluding people in your life, taking care of your health and well-being. Have a teacher help you find a Jewish text about this issue that you can study with a partner or in a group.

WRITE

Write a poem that begins "To be a Jew in the 21st century is ..."
What would you write next?

Here are some questions to get you started on writing in your journal about your Jewish identity.

1. What makes you proud to be a Jew?

2. What embarrasses you about being Jewish?

3. What external signs identify you as a Jew (your clothing, the way you eat, what you read, etc.)?

4. Do you do anything in your life to identify with Israel? What are your feelings about Israel?

5. What has been your most positive experience as a Jew?

6. How does being a Jew make you different from others?

7. What makes you happy to be a Jew? When do you feel excited about your Judaism?

8. What is the most important Jewish symbol for you? Why?

9. Is there anything in your daily life that reminds you and inspires you to be a Jew?

10. Is there anything special about being a Jewish girl?

WOMEN AND TORAH STUDY

M'KOROT

"There are things whose fruits a person eats in this world, while in the world to come a person will reap even more: honoring parents, deeds of lovingkindness, going to the house of study morning and evening, hospitality to guests, visiting the sick, attending a bride, burying the dead, meaningful prayer, making peace between people; but the study of Torah exceeds them all" —Talmud, *Shabbat* 127a

LEARN

In the past few decades there has been an explosion in Torah study for women.

Ask your grandmother or any Jewish woman over 50 what her Jewish education was like. In traditional Jewish households girls were given only a very elementary Hebrew education. Some people felt that giving girls formal Torah study was a waste of time, because their main function in life was to marry and have babies so that the Jewish People could continue. Although many people did not feel this way, this idea was perpetuated over the ages. For centuries women were taught only basic Jewish laws for keeping a household. They were assumed to be knowledgeable about them as early as the Mishnah, written in about 200 C.E. Women were not taught through formal text study, however. Mother passed on the knowledge to daughter, generation after generation.

In addition, most Jewish women did not have time to study Torah the way their husbands did. In eastern Europe, in traditional households, until the 20th century, the woman's role was to support her husband and sons while they studied Torah in the *bet midrash* (house of study). She had to earn a livelihood, bear and raise children, and manage a household.

Now times are different. Today many Jewish girls have a bat mitzvah ceremony and have an opportunity to study Torah in formal settings.

When we talk about *Torah,* we mean one of two things. *Torah* means "instruction" in Hebrew. It specifically refers to the Five Books of Moses, the first five books of the Bible. However, the word can also refer to the collective rabbinic wisdom that serves as commentary to the Bible and that created *halakhah,* or Jewish law. In this sense, studying Talmud is "studying Torah."

The Torah was given to the Jewish People as an instruction manual on how to live in this world, much like the instruction manual you get when you buy a new cell phone or board game. You need to read the manual in order to understand how to use the machine. The Torah contains advice on a whole range of topics, including how to deal with your best friend when you're having a fight, how to communicate better with your parents, health concerns, and peer pressure.

We All Stood Together

My brother and I were at Sinai
He kept a journal
of what he saw
of what he heard
of what it all meant to him

I wish I had such a record
of what happened to me there

It seems like every time I want to write
I can't
I'm always holding a baby
one of my own
or one for a friend
always holding a baby
so my hands are never free
to write things down

And then
as time passes
the particulars
the hard data
the who what when where why
slip away from me
and all I'm left with is
the feeling

But feelings are just sounds
the vowel barking of a mute

My brother is so sure of what he heard
after all he's got a record of it
consonant after consonant after consonant

If we remembered it together
We could recreate holy time
sparks flying

—Merle Feld, *Spiritual Life*

WRITE

According to Midrash, all Jewish souls were present at Mt. Sinai, even those not yet born (*Exodus Rabbah* 28:4). Everyone there received the Torah in their own way, according to their own understanding. It is up to each individual to give their Torah, their personal wisdom, to the world.

Making midrash, creative explanations that fill in the gaps in Torah stories, is something Jewish women still do today. It is an ancient Jewish tradition, an activity in which Jews have always engaged. When we make midrash, we try to understand something in a text in a deeper way. The poem that you just read, Merle Feld's "We All Stood Together," is an example of modern midrash.

You can even make a midrash of your own. Imagine yourself at Sinai. Try to see yourself standing at the foot of the mountain with all the other Jews who had recently escaped from Egypt. The Bible says:

> And it came to pass, that there were thunders and light-ning and a thick cloud upon the mountain, and the sound of a *shofar* exceedingly loud so that all the people in the camp trembled. And Moses brought the people out of the camp to meet with God; and they stood at the foot of the mountain. And Mount Sinai smoked in every part because the Lord descended upon it in fire. And the smoke of it ascended like the smoke of a furnace, and the whole mountain quaked greatly. And then the voice of the *shofar* sounded louder and louder; Moses speaks and God answers him by a voice. —Exodus 19:16–20

Imagine you were there. What were you thinking and feeling as you saw all this? What would you want to write down for your descendants to read so that they could understand what it was like to be there?

Here are some other ideas to get you started writing your own midrash.

- What did Eve say to Adam after God discovered that they had eaten the forbidden fruit?
- You were a little girl at the Sea of Reeds when Moses split it. Describe how you felt.
- Come up with your own story. Think of something that bothers you or intrigues you about the Torah.

Pirkei Banot

"Torah is sometimes referred to in Jewish textual tradition as a path. Study of Torah is for me an attempt to follow that path, which I believe leads toward God. One 20th-century scholar, when asked why he favored brief *davenning* (praying) in order to return more quickly to his studies, is reported to have responded, 'When I pray, I talk to God; when I study, God talks to me.' God's voice echoes through the texts I study, but I don't see study as a one-way street. Studying Torah leads me into a dialogue with God; if God is offering questions and answers, then I too am countering with my own concerns....

"The texts of rabbinic Judaism are the work of men, and the views of women that they offer are frequently disturbing. Furthermore, while women are studying Torah today more than at any other time in Jewish history, the idea of women as students and teachers of Talmud is still bizarre to many and offensive to some....

"I refuse to believe that God avoids women. I believe that God is willing to enter into a relationship with anyone who seeks such a relationship. I also believe that Torah is accessible to all who wish to study it. I am not willing to dismiss texts because parts of them upset me. Traditional texts form the basis of the Judaism of which I want to be a part; can I leave their interpretation to men and then protest that my concerns are not dealt with?" —Talmud professor Dvora Weisberg

Meet

Israeli Bible scholars

Nechamah Leibowitz (1902–1997), one of the first female biblical commentators in the 20th century, was from an illustrious Jerusalemite family of scholars and thinkers. She is known for her popular *gilyonot,* questions to help students of the Bible understand the classical commentators such as Rashi, Ibn Ezra, Abravanel, and Nachmanides.

Avivah Zornberg is a contemporary biblical commentator who grew up in Scotland, daughter of the chief rabbi there. She had an excellent background in Jewish texts and later earned a Ph.D. in English literature from Cambridge University. She has taught Torah to thousands of students in Israel and around the world. When she conducts a class on a specific set of texts, she brings modern and contemporary literature and psychology to bear on them. Her books bring the Bible to life in new ways.

Chanah Henkin is the founder and dean of Nishmat, the Jerusalem Center for Advanced Jewish Studies for Women. She has received awards from the Israel Ministry of Education and from Yeshiva University.

Chana Safrai, professor of Talmud and Jewish history at the Hebrew University of Jerusalem, has written and edited numerous books on rabbinic literature and women's studies. She is coeditor of *Jewish Legal Writings by Women.*

American Rabbis

The first female rabbi ordained in the United States was Sally Priesand, ordained by the Reform movement in 1972. Since then, American female rabbis have been actively involved in a wide range of intellectual quests. Rabbi Sandy Eisenberg Sasso, the first female Reconstructionist rabbi, is an award-winning children's book author who creates new life-cycle rituals for women. She presents meaningful ceremonies filled with texts, songs, and customs for families to do when a baby girl is born. Rabbi Amy Eilberg, the first Conservative female rabbi, is passionate about training women to be spiritual leaders and guides. Deeply concerned with making mysticism and spirituality accessible to women, she teaches small groups of women the texts and practices that have traditionally been reserved for men.

Do It

There is a saying about the Torah, "Turn it and turn it, for everything is in it" (*Pirkei Avot* 5:25). Answers to many of life's questions can be found in the Torah if you know where to look. If you don't know where to look, you can ask someone. Torah study is enhanced when done with a partner—a friend, a teacher, a rabbi. The traditional way of studying Torah is in a *yeshiva,* a special school where you study with a partner. The idea is that both of your minds will stretch by conversing with each other and engaging with the text.

Select a study partner and agree to meet on a regular basis for some period. A good way to find Jewish sources on a particular topic is through *Encyclopedia Judaica,* which is available in most libraries or on CD-ROM, or through one of the websites listed in the Resources. Here are some ideas for topics you might study:

- The environment
- Kindness to animals
- Body image
- Responsibility to the community
- Gossip
- Prayer
- How to improve yourself
- Respecting people your own age
- Love for the Land of Israel
- *Tikkun olam*
- Women in the Torah
- The Jewish holiday cycle

MEET

Sukkot Guests

During the harvest festival of Sukkot, we have a practice called *ush-pizin* (inviting guests). The essence of Sukkot is hospitality. As you sit in your *sukkah,* you are supposed to invite a different guest in each night. Traditionally these guests are Abraham, Isaac, Jacob, Joseph, Moses, Aaron, and King David. Do you notice anything peculiar about this list? That's right—no women.

Now people have began to invite illustrious female ancestors into the *sukkah* as well, women like Sarah, Rebecca, Rachel, Leah, Dinah, Miriam, and Deborah, for instance (you need to pick seven). Since there is no traditional list of women, you can make up your own guest list. This is often the way it is with Jewish women's rituals. So many occasions are just blank slates, because they did not exist for women until very recently. Bat mitzvah ceremonies and the *sukkah* guest list are just two examples.

This is why it is so exciting to be a Jewish girl or woman today. The Jewish community needs you to be an active member, to recognize the need for a certain occasion to be marked that may have been ignored before, or for an aspect of girls' and women's experience to be acknowledged.

Now it is your turn to come up with women and girls who would be good models for this chapter on Jewish identity. Who should be included? What Jewish woman or girl do you know who exemplifies the best there is? Are there women and girls from Jewish history, including the Bible, whom you would include on such a list?

Bible "Babes"

There are many Jewish songwriters who deal with their identity through their music. Remember Adam Sandler's "Chanukah Song"? Rabbi Geela Rayzel Raphael is a musician in the Philadelphia area who has written many songs about Jewish women, especially about women who are not well known. Listen to "Bible Babes a-Beltin'," a title that illustrates her southern Jewish background. You learn about Jewish women you may have never even heard of: Batya, Bat-Yiftach, Ritzpah, Tamar, and Hatzlelponit. Geela Rayzel sings with two other women, who make up the band Miraj. Some of their CDs are *Counting Angels in the Wilderness* and *A Moon Note*. Many of their songs are about Shabbat and holidays and offer new interpretations of Jewish customs.

WRITE

Choose one Jewish woman or girl you would like to introduce to the world, someone who, as a Jew, inspires and teaches you. What about her makes her special to you? Tell a story about her: how you met her, how she has changed your life, something she did that conveys who she is and what you admire about her.

If you want to write about a Jewish woman or girl you have never met, go ahead. What makes you respect her as a Jew? What have you learned from her words and/or actions? Introduce her to the world, describing what makes her exceptional.

FINAL WORDS

Jewish identity is not one thing or one way of being. There are many, many ways to be Jewish. Your own Jewish identity is unique, even as you share a history and a future with other Jews.

Believe it or not, your Jewish identity will change throughout your life. Just as your body changes, so do your beliefs and opinions and your idea of who you are. These things may have changed as you were reading and working with this book. When you were a little girl, your Jewish identity may have been linked with celebrating

Chanukah and Passover with your family. One time Penina's little sister said to a non-Jewish babysitter who told her to get down on her knees and pray before she got into bed, "We don't pray, we're Chanukah."

Now that you are approaching or already in your teens, your notion of Jewish identity is probably becoming more complex. You may really like attending your Passover seder with family and friends. Perhaps you explained parts of it to the people around the seder table. You may be planning a trip to Israel, or to participate in the March of the Living to learn about the Holocaust. You may be going to Jewish summer camp, or participating in Maccabi sports activities or joining a Jewish youth group.

You may also notice that sometimes you feel like an outsider as a Jewish person in America. You may be increasingly aware that you do not belong to the mainstream Christian culture. Instead of church, you may attend synagogue. You may care about the fate of Israel in a personal way that is hard to explain to people who don't feel rooted there. Even if you don't keep strictly kosher, you may not be used to eating ham or bacon or shellfish, or mixing meat and dairy products. Your last name may be difficult for some people to pronounce.

If you are a Sephardi Jew, you are a minority in a minority, for most North American Jews are Ashkenazi. You may not feel like you even belong to a Jewish world at all.

Being Jewish is both a joy and a challenge. Struggle is at the core of the Jewish People, whose name, Israel, means "one who struggles with God." As a Jewish girl on your way to becoming a Jewish woman, you are already struggling to figure out your place in the world. You are struggling to understand what it really means to be a *Jewish* woman rather than any other sort of woman. May your struggle be productive. May it bring you great vitality and an appreciation of life!

Mitzvah g'dolah l'hiyot b'simchah tamid (It is a great mitzvah to be joyful always)! —Rabbi Nachman of Breslov

GLOSSARY

Adonai: Often used to stand in for the name of God, Y-H-V-H, which, according to Jewish teachings, may not be pronounced.

Betzelem Elohim: "In the image of God."

Brit: Covenant, the agreement or "deal" between God and the Jewish people; also, circumcision of male Jews and the celebration associated with that ritual.

G'milut chasadim: "Acts of lovingkindness," showing care and concern for other people.

Hakhnasat orchim: "Welcoming guests."

Kavod habriot: "Honoring all creation."

Kashrut: The traditional Jewish laws and instructions about preparing and eating food.

K'doshim tihyu: "You shall be holy." God instructed the Jewish people to be holy in imitation of the Divine.

K'dushah: "Holiness"; literally means "separation."

Kibud av va'em: "Honoring father and mother."

Kol k'vodah bat melekh p'nimah: "The true majesty of a royal daughter is inside her."

Kol Israel areivim zeh lazeh: "All of Israel are responsible for one another."

Ma'akhil re'eyvim: "Feeding the hungry."

Maimonides: Rabbi Moses ben Maimon, also called Rambam,

lived from 1135 to 1204. He was born in Spain and later moved to Egypt because Jews were being persecuted in Spain. He was the sultan's physician as well as a Jewish philosopher. One of the greatest Jewish scholars, he is the author of the *Guide for the Perplexed* and *Mishneh Torah,* among other works.

Menschlikhkeit: (Yiddish) the quality of being a *mensch,* a moral person who strives to behave properly and treat other people with kindness.

Midrash: Commentary on the Torah that includes creative explanations and stories. The main book of collected *Midrash* is called *Midrash Rabbah.* The word *midrash* is also used to refer to a particular tale or story.

Mikvah: A ritual bath used by both men and women separately for spiritual purification.

Mitzvah (pl. *mitzvot*): A commandment, a law, an element of instruction, or a good deed.

Pikuach nefesh: "Saving a life."

Rashi: Rabbi Shlomo bar Yitzchaki. One of the most important Bible scholars, he lived from 1040 to 1105 and wrote hundreds of commentaries on the Torah. Rashi made Torah learning more accessible to people who were less educated by offering insightful explanations.

Rosh Chodesh: "The head of the month." The first of each Hebrew month is a semi-festival on which special blessings are said. It is has a particularly strong connection with women.

Shmirat halashon: "Guarding your tongue"; the commandment to refrain from gossip, spreading rumors, and speaking negatively about others.

Shmirat Shabbat: Observance of the Sabbath, the seventh day of the week, as a day of rest. A person who observes the Sabbath according to traditional practices is called *shomer Shabbat.*

Shutafey le'ma'aseh bereishit: Being "partners in creation" with God.

T'shuvah: The principle of "turning," to repent and correct our mistakes and wrongdoings.

Tikkun olam: "Repairing the world"; the mitzvah of looking for ways to improve, or fix the problems of, the world.

Tzedakah: Literally, "righteousness"; commonly refers to giving charity.

Tzniut: "Dignity through modesty." This includes the way we dress, eat, speak, and interact with others.

ABOUT THE JEWISH RELIGIOUS MOVEMENTS

There are now four major Jewish religious movements in the United States and Canada. In terms of theology, Reform Judaism is at the liberal end, followed by Reconstructionist, Conservative, and Orthodox—both modern and traditional (which includes several fundamentalist groups, such as the Hasidim).

Reform Judaism, which began in the early 19th century in Germany, regards Judaism as an ongoing process resulting from the relationship between God and the Jewish People over its history. It considers Torah divinely inspired and subject to individual interpretation based on study, and emphasizes the ethical and moral messages of the prophets to help create a just society.

Reconstructionism, founded in the 1930s, is the most recent of the major Jewish movements. Here the essence of Judaism is defined as embodying an entire civilization and not only a religion. At the core of this civilization is a people who have the authority and the responsibility to "reconstruct" its contents from generation to generation.

Conservative Judaism began in the mid-19th century as a reaction to what its founders perceived to be Reform's radicalism. It teaches that while the Torah as a whole is binding and that much of Jewish law remains authoritative, nonetheless new ideas and practices have always influenced Jewish beliefs and rituals and this should continue today as well.

Orthodox Judaism teaches that Torah was divinely revealed to Moses at Mount Sinai and that the *halakhah,* the interpretive process of that law, is both divinely guided and authoritative. Thus, no law stemming from the Torah can be tampered with even if it displeases modern sensibilities. Orthodoxy often rejects more modern forms of Judaism as deviations from divine truths and authentic modes of Jewish life.

For More Information...

The books indicated with an asterisk are great reads even for younger JGirls, ages 11 and under.

Friendship

* American Girl Library. *The Care and Keeping of Friends* (Middleton, Wis.: Pleasant Company, 1996).

Apter, Terri, and Ruthellen Josselson. *Best Friends: The Pleasures and Perils of Girls' and Women's Friendships* (New York: Crown, 1998).

Pipher, Mary. *Reviving Ophelia: Saving the Selves of Adolescent Girls* (New York: Ballantine Books, 2002).

Shandler, Sarah. *Ophelia Speaks: Adolescent Girls Write about Their Search for Self* (New York: Perennial, 1999).

Mitzvot

* Artson, Bradley Shavit. *It's a Mitzvah: Step-by-Step to Jewish Living* (Springfield, N.J.: Behrman House, 1995).

* Feinstein, Edward. *Tough Questions Jews Ask: A Young Adult's Guide to Building a Jewish Life* (Woodstock, Vt.: Jewish Lights, 2003).

Greenberg, Blu. *How to Run a Traditional Jewish Household* (New York: Simon & Schuster, 1985).

Wengrov, Charles, trans. *The Concise Book of Mitzvot: The Commandments Which Can Be Observed Today* (Nanuet, N.Y.: Feldheim, 1990).

Blessings

Falk, Marcia. *The Book of Blessings* (Boston: Beacon Press, 1999).

Kula, Irwin, and Vanessa L. Ochs. *The Book of Jewish Sacred Practices: CLAL's Guide to Everyday and Holiday Rituals and Blessings* (Woodstock, Vt.: Jewish Lights, 2001).

Jewish Identity

* Asher, Sandy, ed. *With All My Heart, with All My Mind: Thirteen Stories about Growing Up Jewish* (New York: Simon & Schuster, 1999).

Frankel, Ellen. *Choosing to Be Chosen: Values through Living* (Jersey City, N.J.: KTAV, 2003).

Green, Arthur. *These Are the Words: A Vocabulary of Jewish Spiritual Life* (Woodstock, Vt.: Jewish Lights, 2000).

Kushner, Lawrence. *The Book of Miracles: A Young Person's Guide to Jewish Spiritual Awareness* (Woodstock, Vt.: Jewish Lights, 1997).

Mack, Stan. *The Story of the Jews: A 4,000-Year Adventure—A Graphic History Book* (Woodstock, Vt.: Jewish Lights, 2001).

Pearl, Judea, and Ruth Pearl, eds. *I Am Jewish: Personal Reflections Inspired by the Last Words of Daniel Pearl* (Woodstock, Vt.: Jewish Lights, 2004).

Telushkin, Rabbi Joseph. *Jewish Literacy: The Most Important Things to Know About the Jewish Religion, Its People and Its History* (New York: William Morrow, 1991).

Tzedakah

* Siegel, Danny. *116 Practical Mitzvah Suggestions* (New York: *Tikkun Olam*, 1997).

*———. *Making a Real Difference in the World: 8 Jewish Texts Teach Us How to Do Tikkun Olam* (New York: *Tikkun Olam*, 1995).

* Ziv Tzedakah Fund, the website for Danny Siegel's *tzedakah* organization (www.ziv.org).

Becoming Bat Mitzvah

Milgram, Goldie. *Make Your Own Bar/Bat Mitzvah: A Personal Guide to a Meaningful Rite of Passage* (San Francisco: Jossey-Bass, 2004).

Leneman, Helen, ed. *Bar/Bat Mitzvah Basics: A Practical Family Guide to Coming of Age Together* (Woodstock, Vt.: Jewish Lights, 1996).

* Salkin, Jeffrey K. *For Kids—Putting God on Your Guest List: How to Claim the Spiritual Meaning of Your Bar or Bat Mitzvah* (Woodstock, Vt.: Jewish Lights, 1998).

Salkin, Jeffrey K., and Nina Salkin. *The Bar/Bat Mitzvah Memory Book: An Album for Treasuring the Spiritual Celebration* (Woodstock, Vt.: Jewish Lights, 2001).

Jewish Women

* Frank, Anne. *The Diary of a Young Girl* (New York: Bantam Books, 1993).

Goldstein, Elyse M. *Seek Her Out: A Textual Approach to the Study of Women and Judaism* (New York: URJ Press, 2004).

* Hillesum, Etty. *An Interrupted Life: The Diaries of Etty Hillesum, 1941–1943* (New York: Pantheon Books, 1983).

Jewish Women's Archive (www.jwa.org), a website full of information about—and writing from—Jewish women throughout history.

Orenstein, Debra, ed. *Lifecycles, Vol. 1: Jewish Women on Life Passages and Personal Milestones* (Woodstock, Vt.: Jewish Lights, 1998).

Orenstein, Debra, and Jane Rachel Litman, eds. *Lifecycles, vol. 2: Jewish Women on Biblical Themes in Contemporary Life* (Woodstock, Vt.: Jewish Lights, 1998).

* Sasso, Sandy Eisenberg. *But God Remembered: Stories of Women from Creation to the Promised Land* (Woodstock, Vt.: Jewish Lights, 1995).

Slater, Elinor, and Robert Slater. *Great Jewish Women* (New York: Jonathan David, 1998).

Torah Study

Bialyk, Hayim, and Yehoshuah Hana Ravnitsky. *The Book of Legends*/Sefer Ha-Aggadah (New York: Schocken Books, 1992).

Frankel, Ellen. *The Five Books of Miriam* (New York: G.P. Putnam's Sons, 1996).

Goldstein, Elyse, ed. *The Women's Torah Commentary: New Insights from Women Rabbis on the 54 Weekly Torah Portions* (Woodstock, Vt.: Jewish Lights, 2000).

————. *The Women's Haftarah Commentary: New Insights from Women Rabbis on the 54 Weekly Haftarah Portions, the 5 Megillot, and Special Shabbatot* (Woodstock, Vt.: Jewish Lights, 2004).

Your Changing Body

Bell, Ruth, ed. *Changing Bodies, Changing Lives: A Book for Teens on Sex and Relationships* (New York: Random House, 1998).

Brumberg, Joan Jacobs. *The Body Project: An Intimate History of American Girls* (New York: Random House, 1997).

Manolson, Gila. *Inside, Outside: A Fresh Look at Tzniut* (Nanuet, N.Y.: Feldheim, 1997).

* Schaefer, Valorie Lee. *The Care and Keeping of You: The Body Book for Girls* (Middleton, Wis.: Pleasant Company, 1998).

Teenwire, a website sponsored by Planned Parenthood (www.teenwire.com/index.asp).

Staying Healthy

* Bodywise, a website sponsored by the U.S. Department of Health and Human Services (www.girlpower.gov).

Covey, Sean. *The 7 Habits of Highly Effective Teens* (New York: Fireside, 1998).

www.freevibe.com, an anti-drug website just for teens.

Gürze Books, on eating disorders, 800-756-7533 or 760-434-7533, e-mail gzcatl@aol.com. www.gurze.net/.

Litapayach Tikvah—To Nourish Hope, a pamphlet created by the Union of American Hebrew Congregations. New York: UAHC, 2000. Available online at www.urj.org/Documents/ index.cfm?id=1855.

National Eating Disorder Association (603 Steward Street, Suite 803, Seattle, WA 98101, 206-382-3587, www.nationaleatingdisorders.org).

Polish, Daniel, Daniel B. Syme, and Bernard M. Zlotowitz. *Drugs, Sex, and Integrity: What Does Judaism Say?* (New York: URJ Press, 1991).

Shabbat

Friedman, Debbie. *Sing Unto God* (audio recording). Available through Sounds Write at www.soundswrite.com.

Lubell, Jonathan. *Shabbat Shalom* (video recording). Jerusalem, Israel: Scopus Productions, 1994.

*Musleah, Rahel, and Michael Klayman. *Sharing Blessings: Children's Stories of Exploring the Spirit of the Jewish Holidays* (Woodstock, Vt.: Jewish Lights, 1997).

Mykoff, Moshe. *Seventh Heaven: Shabbat with Rebbe Nachman of Breslov* (Woodstock, Vt.: Jewish Lights, 2003).

Reider, Freda. *The Hallah Book: Recipes, History and Traditions* (New York: KTAV, 1987).

Shapiro, Mark Dov. *Gates of Shabbat: A Guide for Observing Shabbat* (New York: Central Conference of American Rabbis, 1991).

Wolfson, Ron. *Shabbat, 2nd ed.: The Family Guide to Preparing for and Celebrating the Sabbath* (Woodstock, Vt.: Jewish Lights, 2002).

Smart Fun

Blume, Judy. *Are You There, God? It's Me, Margaret* (New York: Bantam, Doubleday, Dell Publishing Group, 1970).

* Cohn, Janice. *The Christmas Menorahs: How a Town Fought Hate* (Morton Grove, Ill.: Albert Whitman, 1995).

Falon, Janet Ruth. *The Jewish Journaling Book: How to Use Jewish Tradition to Write Your Life & Explore Your Soul* (Woodstock, Vt.: Jewish Lights, 2004).

www.GURL.com, a website for teen girls.

JVibe, a webzine just for Jewish teens (www.jvibe.com).

Levitin, Sonia. *Journey to America* (New York: Scholastic, 1970).

* *New Moon*, the magazine for girls (www.newmoon.org).

Ochs, Vanessa, and Elizabeth Ochs. *The Jewish Dream Book: The Key to Opening the Inner Meaning of Your Dreams* (Woodstock, Vt.: Jewish Lights, 2003).

Rosh Hodesh: It's A Girl Thing! (www.roshhodesh.org), an informal education program that uses Judaism to enrich the lives of girls. Groups meet monthly in locations across North America.

Wolff, Ferida. *Pink Slippers, Bat Mitzvah Blues* (Philadelphia: Jewish Publication Society, 1989).

* Wolff, Virginia Euwer. *The Mozart Season* (New York: Scholastic Books, 1991).

NOTES

Introduction (pp. xvii–xxxvi)

I begin tonight: Excerpted from the May 1, 1861, entry in the diary of Eliza Moses (Sc-8504, American Jewish Archives).

Chapter One (pp. 1–16)

I do not know what's wrong: Excerpted from the November 26, 1890, entry in the diary of Jennie Franklin (American Jewish Archives, MS 502).

Chapter Two (pp. 17–32)

For poor brides who were: This poem by Kadya Molodowsky, "Women-Poems, VI," appears in *Paper Bridges: Selected Poems of Kadya Molodowsky,* edited and translated by Kathryn Hellerstein (Detroit: Wayne State University Press, 1999), 79.

Chapter Three (pp. 33–51)

The dishes of my aunt Latifa and her cook Nessim: This excerpt was taken from *The Book of Jewish Food: An Odyssey from Samarkand to New York* by Claudia Roden (New York: Alfred A. Knopf, 1996), 569.

Invite people living in your community who: These activities are excerpted from *Jewish Family & Life: Traditions, Holidays, and Values for Today's Parents and Children* by Yosef Abramowitz and Susan Silverman (New York: Golden Guides from St. Martin's Press, 1998), 124.

It wasn't about dishes, or law: This excerpt was taken from *Miriam's Kitchen* by Elizabeth Ehrlich (New York: Viking, 1997), 127.

My mother grew up in a very religious home: This quotation by Karen Erdos is from Ellen Umansky and Dianne Ashton's *Four Centuries of Jewish Women's Spirituality* (Boston: Beacon Press, 1992), 308.

Before I respond to the growl in my stomach: This quotation comes from *Jewish Family & Life: Traditions, Holidays, and Values for Today's Parents and Children* by Yosef Abramowitz and Susan Silverman (New York: Golden Guides from St. Martin's Press, 1998), 124.

An eating disorder is not about food: This quotation from Rabbi Jennifer Rebecca Marx was cited by Rabbi Janet Marder in her sermon "All Who Are Hungry," March 31, 2004. This sermon is available online at www.betham.org/sermons/marder040331.html.

In the world of adolescent girls: This excerpt comes from *Ophelia Speaks: Adolescent Girls Write about Their Search for Self,* edited by Sarah Shandler (New York: Perennial, 1999), 12.

Chapter Four (pp. 52–70)

set apart one day a week: This excerpt comes from *The Sabbath: Its Meaning for Modern Man,* by Abraham Joshua Heschel (New York: Farrar, Straus and Giroux, 1951), 28.

Shabbat adds a sweetness and a rhythm: This excerpt comes from *It's a Mitzvah,* by Bradley Shavit Artson (New Jersey: Berhman House, 1995), 134.

The Sabbath began: This text is reprinted from Jennie Rosenfeld Gerstley's *"Reminiscences"—of Chicago in the 1860s and 1870s* (American Jewish Archives, Box 2072).

At dusk, I kindled four candles: This poem by Kadya Molodowsky, "Sabbath Song," appears in *Paper Bridges: Selected Poems of Kadya*

Molodowsky, edited and translated by Kathryn Hellerstein (Detroit: Wayne State University Press, 1999), 453 and 455.

The women gathered for prayer: This text is reprinted from Malkah Shapiro's *The Rebbe's Daughter: Memoirs of a Hasidic Girl in Poland before World War II* (Philadelphia: Jewish Publication Society, 2001), 66.

FAQs about Shabbat: Reprinted from *Every Persons' Guide to Shabbat* by Ronald H. Isaacs (Northvale, N.J.: Jason Aronson, 1998), 103–109.

lead prayers and Torah discussion themselves on Shabbat: For more about this movement, see *The First Jewish Catalogue* by Michael and Sharon Strassfeld (Philadelphia: Jewish Publication Society, 1976).

I met my friend Eleanor: From a personal communication from Boorstein to the authors.

Make your own braided havdalah candle: This activity, created by Rebecca E. Kotkin, is excerpted from http://jewishfamily.com/jc/holidays/havdalah_with_a.txt.

Chapter Five (pp. 71–83)

Do you know about all these Jewish female athletes?: This list is from a letter to the editor of the *Foreword* by Nancy Vineberg.

an activity entitled "Baby Steps": Based on text from *The 7 Habits of Highly Effective Teens* by Sean Covey (New York: Fireside, 1998).

Chapter Six (pp. 84–98)

according to author Gila Manolson: For more on this, see *Inside, Outside: A Fresh Look at* Tzniut, by Gila Manolson (Nanuet, N.Y.: Feldheim, 1997), 25.

with puberty, girls face: This quotation comes from *Reviving Ophelia: Saving the Selves of Adolescent Girls,* by Mary Pipher (New York: Ballantine Books, 2002), 38.

Got new hat and shoes yesterday: Excerpted from the April 19, 1896, entry in the diary of Bella Weretnikow, 17, Seattle (American Jewish Archives, MS 179).

Tues., 1 August 1944.... Excerpted from *The Diary of a Young Girl* by Anne Frank (New York: Bantam Books, 1993), 266.

Once upon a time, there was a prince: For the original story, see "The Turkey Prince" in *The Seven Beggars & Other Kabbalistic Tales of Rebbe Nachman of Breslov,* translated and with annotations by Rabbi Aryeh Kaplan; introduction by Rabbi Chaim Kramer (Woodstock, Vt.: Jewish Lights, 2005).

Chapter Seven (pp. 99–119)

Welcome to the sisterhood: This ritual has been adapted from Rabbi Goldie Milgram's "Ritual for Welcoming Bodily Change," available at www.RitualWell.org.

Rabbi Goldstein's revised version allows: This blessing initially appeared in *Lilith* (Spring 1990), 32.

When I was a freshman in college: Excerpted from *Celebrating Our Cycles: A Jewish Woman's Introduction to Menstruation and Womanhood* by Rachel Shnider (Waltham, Mass.: Hadassah-Brandeis Institute, 2002).

It makes sense to begin with: This quotation comes from *Like Bread on the Seder Plate: Jewish Lesbians and the Transformation of Tradition* by Rebecca Alpert (New York: Columbia University Press, 1997), 54.

Touching inappropriately: This list is from "Know Your Rights," *Teen Voices,* 9:2 (2000), 35.

Chapter Eight (pp. 120–133)

Gracious and merciful God: This text is quoted from *It's a Mitzvah* by Bradley Shavit Artson (Springfield, N.J.: Behrman House, 1995), 153.

Once there was a woman who said awful things about another person: This retelling is inspired by *Yettele's Feathers* by Joan Rothenberg (New York: Hyperion Paperbacks, 1996).

We abuse, we betray, we are cruel: This translation is from the New York Rabbinical Assembly *Mahzor* for Rosh Hashanah and Yom Kippur, 1972, 1978.

Chapter Nine (pp. 134–148)

Here are some ideas: This list was taken in part from *116 Practical Mitzvah Suggestions* by Danny Siegel (New York: *Tikun Olam,* 1997).

It was young Jewish women in their teens: This text was written by Michele Landsberg, columnist for the *Toronto Star.* It appeared on March 8, 1997.

I was reared in a traditional Jewish household: This quote comes from "Alicia Silverstone's Most Ambitious Role Ever," an article written by Ivor Davis and available online at www.jvibe.com/popculture/stone.shtml.

Sitting in synagogue, singing songs, it's a very close, warm feeling: From a Prodigy Online Chat, 1997, available online at www.allaboutalicia.com/alicia/chat/prodigy.html.

Chapter Ten (pp. 149–170)

Dear Mr. Benedict: This letter comes from *Are You There, God? It's Me, Margaret* by Judy Blume (New York: Bantam, Doubleday, Dell, 1970), 142–143.

Letter to the Front: This poem, called "Letter to the Front," was written by Muriel Rukeyser. It appears in her book *The Collected Poems* (New York: McGraw Hill, 1978), 239.

We All Stood Together: This poem, called "We All Stood Together," was written by Merle Feld. It appears in her book *Spiritual Life* (Albany: State University of New York Press, 1999), 205.

Torah is sometimes referred to in Jewish textual tradition: This quotation by Dvora Weisberg is from Ellen Umansky and Dianne Ashton's *Four Centuries of Jewish Women's Spirituality* (Boston: Beacon Press, 1992), 276–278.

About the Jewish Religous Movements (pp. 174–175)

There are now four major Jewish religious movements: This text comes from *How to Be a Perfect Stranger, 3rd Edition: The Essential Religious Etiquette Handbook* (Woodstock, Vt.: SkyLight Paths, 2002), 133.

My Thoughts

MY THOUGHTS

Children's Books

What You Will See Inside a Synagogue
By Rabbi Lawrence A. Hoffman and Dr. Ron Wolfson; Full-color photos by Bill Aron

A colorful, fun-to-read introduction that explains the ways and whys of Jewish worship and religious life. Full-page photos; concise but informative descriptions of the objects used, the clergy and laypeople who have specific roles, and much more. For ages 6 & up.

8½ x 10½, 32 pp, Full-color photos, Hardcover, ISBN 1-59473-012-1 **$17.99** *(A SkyLight Paths book)*

Because Nothing Looks Like God
By Lawrence and Karen Kushner

What is God like? Introduces children to the possibilities of spiritual life. Real-life examples of happiness and sadness invite us to explore, together with our children, the questions we all have about God.

11 x 8½, 32 pp, Full-color illus., Hardcover, ISBN 1-58023-092-X **$16.95** *For ages 4 & up*

Also Available: **Because Nothing Looks Like God Teacher's Guide**
8½ x 11, 22 pp, PB, ISBN 1-58023-140-3 **$6.95** *For ages 5–8*

Board Book Companions to *Because Nothing Looks Like God*
5 x 5, 24 pp, Full-color illus., SkyLight Paths Board Books, **$7.95** each *For ages 0–4*

What Does God Look Like? ISBN 1-893361-23-3
How Does God Make Things Happen? ISBN 1-893361-24-1
Where Is God? ISBN 1-893361-17-9

The 11th Commandment: Wisdom from Our Children
by The Children of America

"If there were an Eleventh Commandment, what would it be?" Children of many religious denominations across America answer in their own drawings and words.

8 x 10, 48 pp, Full-color illus., Hardcover, ISBN 1-879045-46-X **$16.95** *For all ages*

Jerusalem of Gold: Jewish Stories of the Enchanted City
Retold by Howard Schwartz. Full-color illus. by Neil Waldman.

A beautiful and engaging collection of historical and legendary stories for children. Based on Talmud, midrash, Jewish folklore, and mystical and Hasidic sources.

8 x 10, 64 pp, Full-color illus., Hardcover, ISBN 1-58023-149-7 **$18.95** *For ages 7 & up*

The Book of Miracles: A Young Person's Guide to Jewish Spiritual Awareness
By Lawrence Kushner. All-new illustrations by the author.

6 x 9, 96 pp, 2-color illus., Hardcover, ISBN 1-879045-78-8 **$16.95** *For ages 9–13*

In Our Image: God's First Creatures
By Nancy Sohn Swartz

9 x 12, 32 pp, Full-color illus., Hardcover, ISBN 1-879045-99-0 **$16.95** *For ages 4 & up*

Also Available as a Board Book: **How Did the Animals Help God?**
5 x 5, 24 pp, Board, Full-color illus., ISBN 1-59473-044-X **$7.99** *For ages 0–4 (A SkyLight Paths book)*

From SKYLIGHT PATHS PUBLISHING

Becoming Me: A Story of Creation
By Martin Boroson. Full-color illus. by Christopher Gilvan-Cartwright.

Told in the personal "voice" of the Creator, a story about creation and relationship that is about each one of us.

8 x 10, 32 pp, Full-color illus., Hardcover, ISBN 1-893361-11-X **$16.95** *For ages 4 & up*

Ten Amazing People: And How They Changed the World
By Maura D. Shaw. Foreword by Dr. Robert Coles. Full-color illus. by Stephen Marchesi.

Black Elk • Dorothy Day • Malcolm X • Mahatma Gandhi • Martin Luther King, Jr. • Mother Teresa • Janusz Korczak • Desmond Tutu • Thich Nhat Hanh • Albert Schweitzer.

8½ x 11, 48 pp, Full-color illus., Hardcover, ISBN 1-893361-47-0 **$17.95** *For ages 7 & up*

Where Does God Live? *By August Gold and Matthew J. Perlman*
Helps young readers develop a personal understanding of God.

10 x 8½, 32 pp, Full-color photo illus., Quality PB, ISBN 1-893361-39-X **$8.99** *For ages 3–6*

Meditation

The Handbook of Jewish Meditation Practices
A Guide for Enriching the Sabbath and Other Days of Your Life
By Rabbi David A. Cooper
Easy-to-learn meditation techniques. 6 x 9, 208 pp, Quality PB, ISBN 1-58023-102-0 **$16.95**

Discovering Jewish Meditation: Instruction & Guidance for Learning an Ancient
Spiritual Practice *By Nan Fink Gefen, Ph.D.* 6 x 9, 208 pp, Quality PB, ISBN 1-58023-067-9 **$16.95**

A Heart of Stillness: A Complete Guide to Learning the Art of Meditation
By Rabbi David A. Cooper 5½ x 8½, 272 pp, Quality PB, ISBN 1-893361-03-9 **$16.95**
(A SkyLight Paths book)

Meditation from the Heart of Judaism: Today's Teachers Share Their
Practices, Techniques, and Faith *Edited by Avram Davis*
6 x 9, 256 pp, Quality PB, ISBN 1-58023-049-0 **$16.95**

Silence, Simplicity & Solitude: A Complete Guide to Spiritual Retreat at Home
By Rabbi David A. Cooper 5½ x 8½, 336 pp, Quality PB, ISBN 1-893361-04-7 **$16.95**
(A SkyLight Paths book)

The Way of Flame: A Guide to the Forgotten Mystical Tradition of Jewish
Meditation *By Avram Davis* 4½ x 8, 176 pp, Quality PB, ISBN 1-58023-060-1 **$15.95**

Ritual/Sacred Practice/Journaling

The Jewish Dream Book: The Key to Opening the Inner Meaning of
Your Dreams *By Vanessa L. Ochs with Elizabeth Ochs; Full-color illus. by Kristina Swarner*
Instructions for how modern people can perform ancient Jewish dream practices
and dream interpretations drawn from the Jewish wisdom tradition. For anyone
who wants to understand their dreams—and themselves.
8 x 8, 120 pp, Full-color illus., Deluxe PB w/flaps, ISBN 1-58023-132-2 **$16.95**

The Jewish Journaling Book: How to Use Jewish Tradition to Write
Your Life & Explore Your Soul *By Janet Ruth Falon*
Details the history of Jewish journaling throughout biblical and modern times,
and teaches specific journaling techniques to help you create and maintain a vital
journal, from a Jewish perspective. 8 x 8, 304 pp, Deluxe PB w/flaps, ISBN 1-58023-203-5 **$18.99**

The Book of Jewish Sacred Practices: CLAL's Guide to Everyday & Holiday
Rituals & Blessings *Edited by Rabbi Irwin Kula and Vanessa L. Ochs, Ph.D.*
6 x 9, 368 pp, Quality PB, ISBN 1-58023-152-7 **$18.95**

Jewish Ritual: A Brief Introduction for Christians
By Rabbi Kerry M. Olitzky and Rabbi Daniel Judson
5½ x 8½, 144 pp, Quality PB, ISBN 1-58023-210-8 **$14.99**

The Rituals & Practices of a Jewish Life: A Handbook for Personal Spiritual
Renewal *Edited by Rabbi Kerry M. Olitzky and Rabbi Daniel Judson*
6 x 9, 272 pp, illus., Quality PB, ISBN 1-58023-169-1 **$18.95**

Science Fiction/
Mystery & Detective Fiction

Mystery Midrash: An Anthology of Jewish Mystery & Detective Fiction
Edited by Lawrence W. Raphael. Preface by Joel Siegel.
6 x 9, 304 pp, Quality PB, ISBN 1-58023-055-5 **$16.95**

Criminal Kabbalah: An Intriguing Anthology of Jewish Mystery & Detective Fiction
Edited by Lawrence W. Raphael. Foreword by Laurie R. King.
6 x 9, 256 pp, Quality PB, ISBN 1-58023-109-8 **$16.95**

More Wandering Stars: An Anthology of Outstanding Stories of Jewish Fantasy and
Science Fiction *Edited by Jack Dann. Introduction by Isaac Asimov.*
6 x 9, 192 pp, Quality PB, ISBN 1-58023-063-6 **$16.95**

Wandering Stars: An Anthology of Jewish Fantasy & Science Fiction
Edited by Jack Dann. Introduction by Isaac Asimov.
6 x 9, 272 pp, Quality PB, ISBN 1-58023-005-9 **$16.95**

Spirituality/The Way Into... Series

The Way Into... Series offers an accessible and highly usable "guided tour" of the Jewish faith, people, history and beliefs—in total, an introduction to Judaism that will enable you to understand and interact with the sacred texts of the Jewish tradition. Each volume is written by a leading contemporary scholar and teacher, and explores one key aspect of Judaism. The Way Into... enables all readers to achieve a real sense of Jewish cultural literacy through guided study.

The Way Into Encountering God in Judaism By Neil Gillman
6 x 9, 240 pp, Quality PB, ISBN 1-58023-199-3 **$18.99**; Hardcover, ISBN 1-58023-025-3 **$21.95**

Also Available: **The Jewish Approach to God: A Brief Introduction for Christians**
By Neil Gillman 5½ x 8½, 192 pp, Quality PB, ISBN 1-58023-190-X **$16.95**

The Way Into Jewish Mystical Tradition By Lawrence Kushner
6 x 9, 224 pp, Quality PB, ISBN 1-58023-200-0 **$18.99**; Hardcover, ISBN 1-58023-029-6 **$21.95**

The Way Into Jewish Prayer By Lawrence A. Hoffman
6 x 9, 224 pp, Quality PB, ISBN 1-58023-201-9 **$18.99**; Hardcover, ISBN 1-58023-027-X **$21.95**

The Way Into Tikkun Olam By Elliot N. Dorff
6 x 9, 336 pp, Hardcover, ISBN 1-58023-269-8 **$24.99**

The Way Into Torah By Norman J. Cohen
6 x 9, 176 pp, Quality PB, ISBN 1-58023-198-5 **$16.99**; Hardcover, ISBN 1-58023-028-8 **$21.95**

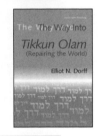 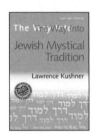  

Spirituality in the Workplace

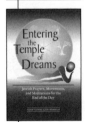

Being God's Partner
How to Find the Hidden Link Between Spirituality and Your Work
By Rabbi Jeffrey K. Salkin. Introduction by Norman Lear.
6 x 9, 192 pp, Quality PB, ISBN 1-879045-65-6 **$17.95**

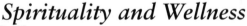

Spirituality and Wellness

Aleph-Bet Yoga
Embodying the Hebrew Letters for Physical and Spiritual Well-Being
By Steven A. Rapp. Foreword by Tamar Frankiel, Ph.D., and Judy Greenfeld. Preface by Hart Lazer
7 x 10, 128 pp, b/w photos, Quality PB, Layflat binding, ISBN 1-58023-162-4 **$16.95**

Entering the Temple of Dreams
Jewish Prayers, Movements, and Meditations for the End of the Day
By Tamar Frankiel, Ph.D., and Judy Greenfeld
7 x 10, 192 pp, illus., Quality PB, ISBN 1-58023-079-2 **$16.95**

Jewish Paths toward Healing and Wholeness: A Personal Guide to Dealing with Suffering By Rabbi Kerry M. Olitzky. Foreword by Debbie Friedman.
6 x 9, 192 pp, Quality PB, ISBN 1-58023-068-7 **$15.95**

Minding the Temple of the Soul
Balancing Body, Mind, and Spirit through Traditional Jewish Prayer, Movement, and Meditation By Tamar Frankiel, Ph.D., and Judy Greenfeld
7 x 10, 184 pp, illus., Quality PB, ISBN 1-879045-64-8 **$16.95**
Audiotape of the Blessings and Meditations: 60 min. **$9.95**
Videotape of the Movements and Meditations: 46 min. **$20.00**

Spirituality/Lawrence Kushner

Filling Words with Light: Hasidic and Mystical Reflections on Jewish Prayer
By Lawrence Kushner and Nehemia Polen
Reflects on the joy, gratitude, mystery and awe embedded in traditional prayers and blessings, and shows how you can imbue these familiar sacred words with your own sense of holiness. 5½ x 8¼, 176 pp, Hardcover, ISBN 1-58023-216-7 **$21.99**

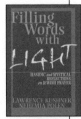

The Book of Letters: A Mystical Hebrew Alphabet
Popular Hardcover Edition, 6 x 9, 80 pp, 2-color text, ISBN 1-879045-00-1 **$24.95**
Collector's Limited Edition, 9 x 12, 80 pp, gold foil embossed pages, w/limited edition silkscreened print, ISBN 1-879045-04-4 **$349.00**

The Book of Miracles: A Young Person's Guide to Jewish Spiritual Awareness
6 x 9, 96 pp, 2-color illus., Hardcover, ISBN 1-879045-78-8 **$16.95** *For ages 9–13*

The Book of Words: Talking Spiritual Life, Living Spiritual Talk
6 x 9, 160 pp, Quality PB, ISBN 1-58023-020-2 **$16.95**

Eyes Remade for Wonder: A Lawrence Kushner Reader *Introduction by Thomas Moore*
6 x 9, 240 pp, Quality PB, ISBN 1-58023-042-3 **$18.95;** Hardcover, ISBN 1-58023-014-8 **$23.95**

God Was in This Place & I, i Did Not Know
Finding Self, Spirituality and Ultimate Meaning 6 x 9, 192 pp, Quality PB, ISBN 1-879045-33-8 **$16.95**

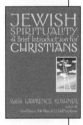

Honey from the Rock: An Introduction to Jewish Mysticism
6 x 9, 176 pp, Quality PB, ISBN 1-58023-073-3 **$16.95**

Invisible Lines of Connection: Sacred Stories of the Ordinary
5½ x 8¼, 160 pp, Quality PB, ISBN 1-879045-98-2 **$15.95**

Jewish Spirituality—A Brief Introduction for Christians
5½ x 8¼, 112 pp, Quality PB Original, ISBN 1-58023-150-0 **$12.95**

The River of Light: Jewish Mystical Awareness 6 x 9, 192 pp, Quality PB, ISBN 1-58023-096-2 **$16.95**

The Way Into Jewish Mystical Tradition
6 x 9, 224 pp, Quality PB, ISBN 1-58023-200-0 **$18.99;** Hardcover, ISBN 1-58023-029-6 **$21.95**

Spirituality/Prayer

Pray Tell: A Hadassah Guide to Jewish Prayer
By Rabbi Jules Harlow, with contributions from Tamara Cohen, Rochelle Furstenberg, Rabbi Daniel Gordis, Leora Tanenbaum, and many others
Enriched with insight and wisdom from a broad variety of viewpoints.
8½ x 11, 400 pp, Quality PB, ISBN 1-58023-163-2 **$29.95**

My People's Prayer Book Series

Traditional Prayers, Modern Commentaries *Edited by Rabbi Lawrence A. Hoffman*
Provides diverse and exciting commentary to the traditional liturgy, helping modern men and women find new wisdom in Jewish prayer, and bring liturgy into their lives. Each book includes Hebrew text, modern translation, and commentaries from all perspectives of the Jewish world.

Vol. 1—The *Sh'ma* and Its Blessings
7 x 10, 168 pp, Hardcover, ISBN 1-879045-79-6 **$24.99**
Vol. 2—The *Amidah*
7 x 10, 240 pp, Hardcover, ISBN 1-879045-80-X **$24.95**
Vol. 3—*P'sukei D'zimrah* (Morning Psalms)
7 x 10, 240 pp, Hardcover, ISBN 1-879045-81-8 **$24.95**
Vol. 4—*Seder K'riat Hatorah* (The Torah Service)
7 x 10, 264 pp, Hardcover, ISBN 1-879045-82-6 **$23.95**
Vol. 5—*Birkhot Hashachar* (Morning Blessings)
7 x 10, 240 pp, Hardcover, ISBN 1-879045-83-4 **$24.95**
Vol. 6—*Tachanun* and Concluding Prayers
7 x 10, 240 pp, Hardcover, ISBN 1-879045-84-2 **$24.95**
Vol. 7—Shabbat at Home
7 x 10, 240 pp, Hardcover, ISBN 1-879045-85-0 **$24.95**
Vol. 8—*Kabbalat Shabbat* (Welcoming Shabbat in the Synagogue)
7 x 10, 240 pp, Hardcover, ISBN 1-58023-121-7 **$24.99**
Vol. 9—Welcoming the Night: *Minchah* and *Ma'ariv* (Afternoon and Evening Prayer) 7 x 10, 272 pp, Hardcover, ISBN 1-58023-262-0 **$24.99**

Spirituality

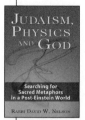

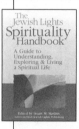

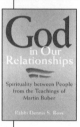

Does the Soul Survive?: A Jewish Journey to Belief in Afterlife, Past Lives & Living with Purpose *By Rabbi Elie Kaplan Spitz. Foreword by Brian L. Weiss, M.D.*
Spitz relates his own experiences and those shared with him by people he has worked with as a rabbi, and shows us that belief in afterlife and past lives, so often approached with reluctance, is in fact true to Jewish tradition.
6 x 9, 288 pp, Quality PB, ISBN 1-58023-165-9 **$16.95**; Hardcover, ISBN 1-58023-094-6 **$21.95**

First Steps to a New Jewish Spirit: Reb Zalman's Guide to Recapturing the Intimacy & Ecstasy in Your Relationship with God
By Rabbi Zalman M. Schachter-Shalomi with Donald Gropman
An extraordinary spiritual handbook that restores psychic and physical vigor by introducing us to new models and alternative ways of practicing Judaism. Offers meditation and contemplation exercises for enriching the most important aspects of everyday life. 6 x 9, 144 pp, Quality PB, ISBN 1-58023-182-9 **$16.95**

God in Our Relationships: Spirituality between People from the Teachings of Martin Buber *By Rabbi Dennis S. Ross*
On the eightieth anniversary of Buber's classic work, we can discover new answers to critical issues in our lives. Inspiring examples from Ross's own life—as congregational rabbi, father, hospital chaplain, social worker, and husband—illustrate Buber's difficult-to-understand ideas about how we encounter God and each other. 5½ x 8½, 160 pp, Quality PB, ISBN 1-58023-147-0 **$16.95**

Judaism, Physics and God: Searching for Sacred Metaphors in a Post-Einstein World *By Rabbi David W. Nelson*
In clear, non-technical terms, this provocative fusion of religion and science examines the great theories of modern physics to find new ways for contemporary people to express their spiritual beliefs and thoughts.
6 x 9, 352 pp, Hardcover, ISBN 1-58023-252-3 **$24.99**

The Jewish Lights Spirituality Handbook: A Guide to Understanding, Exploring & Living a Spiritual Life *Edited by Stuart M. Matlins*
What exactly is "Jewish" about spirituality? How do I make it a part of my life? Fifty of today's foremost spiritual leaders share their ideas and experience with us.
6 x 9, 456 pp, Quality PB, ISBN 1-58023-093-8 **$19.95**; Hardcover, ISBN 1-58023-100-4 **$24.95**

Bringing the Psalms to Life: How to Understand and Use the Book of Psalms
By Dr. Daniel F. Polish
6 x 9, 208 pp, Quality PB, ISBN 1-58023-157-8 **$16.95**; Hardcover, ISBN 1-58023-077-6 **$21.95**

God & the Big Bang: Discovering Harmony between Science & Spirituality
By Dr. Daniel C. Matt 6 x 9, 216 pp, Quality PB, ISBN 1-879045-89-3 **$16.95**

Godwrestling—Round 2: Ancient Wisdom, Future Paths
By Rabbi Arthur Waskow 6 x 9, 352 pp, Quality PB, ISBN 1-879045-72-9 **$18.95**

One God Clapping: The Spiritual Path of a Zen Rabbi *By Rabbi Alan Lew with Sherril Jaffe*
5½ x 8½, 336 pp, Quality PB, ISBN 1-58023-115-2 **$16.95**

The Path of Blessing: Experiencing the Energy and Abundance of the Divine
By Rabbi Marcia Prager 5½ x 8½, 240 pp., Quality PB, ISBN 1-58023-148-9 **$16.95**

Six Jewish Spiritual Paths: A Rationalist Looks at Spirituality *By Rabbi Rifat Sonsino*
6 x 9, 208 pp, Quality PB, ISBN 1-58023-167-5 **$16.95**; Hardcover, ISBN 1-58023-095-4 **$21.95**

Soul Judaism: Dancing with God into a New Era
By Rabbi Wayne Dosick 5½ x 8½, 304 pp, Quality PB, ISBN 1-58023-053-9 **$16.95**

Stepping Stones to Jewish Spiritual Living: Walking the Path Morning, Noon, and Night *By Rabbi James L. Mirel and Karen Bonnell Werth*
6 x 9, 240 pp, Quality PB, ISBN 1-58023-074-1 **$16.95**; Hardcover, ISBN 1-58023-003-2 **$21.95**

There Is No Messiah... and You're It: The Stunning Transformation of Judaism's Most Provocative Idea *By Rabbi Robert N. Levine, D.D.*
6 x 9, 192 pp, Quality PB, ISBN 1-58023-255-8 **$16.99**; Hardcover, ISBN 1-58023-173-X **$21.95**

These Are the Words: A Vocabulary of Jewish Spiritual Life *By Dr. Arthur Green*
6 x 9, 304 pp, Quality PB, ISBN 1-58023-107-1 **$18.95**

Inspiration

God in All Moments
Mystical & Practical Spiritual Wisdom from Hasidic Masters
Edited and translated by Or N. Rose with Ebn D. Leader
Hasidic teachings on how to be mindful in religious practice and cultivating every-day ethical behavior—*hanhagot*. 5½ x 8½, 192 pp, Quality PB, ISBN 1-58023-186-1 **$16.95**

Our Dance with God: Finding Prayer, Perspective and Meaning in the Stories of Our Lives *By Karyn D. Kedar*
Inspiring spiritual insight to guide you on your life journeys and teach you to live and thrive in two conflicting worlds: the rational/material and the spiritual.
6 x 9, 176 pp, Quality PB, ISBN 1-58023-202-7 **$16.99**

Also Available: **The Dance of the Dolphin** (Hardcover edition of *Our Dance with God*)
6 x 9, 176 pp, Hardcover, ISBN 1-58023-154-3 **$19.95**

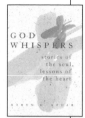

The Empty Chair: Finding Hope and Joy—Timeless Wisdom from a Hasidic Master, Rebbe Nachman of Breslov *Adapted by Moshe Mykoff and the Breslov Research Institute*
4 x 6, 128 pp, 2-color text, Deluxe PB w/flaps, ISBN 1-879045-67-2 **$9.95**

The Gentle Weapon: Prayers for Everyday and Not-So-Everyday Moments—
Timeless Wisdom from the Teachings of the Hasidic Master, Rebbe Nachman of Breslov
Adapted by Moshe Mykoff and S. C. Mizrahi, together with the Breslov Research Institute
4 x 6, 144 pp, 2-color text, Deluxe PB w/flaps, ISBN 1-58023-022-9 **$9.95**

God Whispers: Stories of the Soul, Lessons of the Heart *By Karyn D. Kedar*
6 x 9, 176 pp, Quality PB, ISBN 1-58023-088-1 **$15.95**

An Orphan in History: One Man's Triumphant Search for His Jewish Roots
By Paul Cowan. Afterword by Rachel Cowan. 6 x 9, 288 pp, Quality PB, ISBN 1-58023-135-7 **$16.95**

Restful Reflections: Nighttime Inspiration to Calm the Soul, Based on Jewish Wisdom
By Rabbi Kerry M. Olitzky & Rabbi Lori Forman 4½ x 6½, 448 pp, Quality PB, ISBN 1-58023-091-1 **$15.95**

Sacred Intentions: Daily Inspiration to Strengthen the Spirit, Based on Jewish Wisdom
By Rabbi Kerry M. Olitzky and Rabbi Lori Forman 4½ x 6½, 448 pp, Quality PB, ISBN 1-58023-061-X **$15.95**

Kabbalah/Mysticism/Enneagram

Seek My Face: A Jewish Mystical Theology
By Dr. Arthur Green
This classic work of contemporary Jewish theology, revised and updated, is a pro-found, deeply personal statement of the lasting truths of Jewish mysticism and the basic faith claims of Judaism. A tool for anyone seeking the elusive presence of God in the world. 6 x 9, 304 pp, Quality PB, ISBN 1-58023-130-6 **$19.95**

Zohar: Annotated & Explained
Translation and annotation by Dr. Daniel C. Matt. Foreword by Andrew Harvey
Offers insightful yet unobtrusive commentary to the masterpiece of Jewish mys-ticism. Explains references and mystical symbols, shares wisdom of spiritual mas-ters, and clarifies the *Zohar's* bold claim: We have always been taught that we need God, but in order to manifest in the world, God needs us.
5½ x 8½, 160 pp, Quality PB, ISBN 1-893361-51-9 **$15.99** *(A SkyLight Paths book)*

Cast in God's Image: Discover Your Personality Type Using the Enneagram and Kabbalah
By Rabbi Howard A. Addison
7 x 9, 176 pp, Quality PB, Layflat binding, 20+ journaling exercises, ISBN 1-58023-124-1 **$16.95**

Ehyeh: A Kabbalah for Tomorrow *By Dr. Arthur Green*
6 x 9, 224 pp, Quality PB, ISBN 1-58023-213-2 **$16.99**; Hardcover, ISBN 1-58023-125-X **$21.95**

The Enneagram and Kabbalah: Reading Your Soul *By Rabbi Howard A. Addison*
6 x 9, 176 pp, Quality PB, ISBN 1-58023-001-6 **$15.95**

Finding Joy: A Practical Spiritual Guide to Happiness *By Dannel I. Schwartz with Mark Hass*
6 x 9, 192 pp, Quality PB, ISBN 1-58023-009-1 **$14.95**

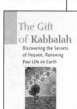

The Gift of Kabbalah: Discovering the Secrets of Heaven, Renewing Your Life on Earth
By Tamar Frankiel, Ph.D.
6 x 9, 256 pp, Quality PB, ISBN 1-58023-141-1 **$16.95**; Hardcover, ISBN 1-58023-108-X **$21.95**

The Way Into Jewish Mystical Tradition *By Lawrence Kushner*
6 x 9, 224 pp, Quality PB, ISBN 1-58023-200-0 **$18.99**; Hardcover, ISBN 1-58023-029-6 **$21.95**

Holidays/Holy Days

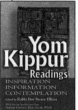

Yom Kippur Readings: Inspiration, Information and Contemplation
Edited by Rabbi Dov Peretz Elkins with section introductions from Arthur Green's These Are the Words
An extraordinary collection of readings, prayers and insights that enable the modern worshiper to enter into the spirit of the Day of Atonement in a personal and powerful way, permitting the meaning of Yom Kippur to enter the heart.
6 x 9, 348 pp, Hardcover, ISBN 1-58023-271-X **$24.99**

Leading the Passover Journey
The Seder's Meaning Revealed, the Haggadah's Story Retold
By Rabbi Nathan Laufer
Uncovers the hidden meaning of the Seder's rituals and customs
6 x 9, 208 pp, Hardcover, ISBN 1-58023-211-6 **$24.99**

Reclaiming Judaism as a Spiritual Practice: Holy Days and Shabbat
By Rabbi Goldie Milgram
Provides a framework for understanding the powerful and often unexplained intellectual, emotional, and spiritual tools that are essential for a lively, relevant, and fulfilling Jewish spiritual practice. 7 x 9, 272 pp, Quality PB, ISBN 1-58023-205-1 **$19.99**

7th Heaven: Celebrating Shabbat with Rebbe Nachman of Breslov
By Moshe Mykoff with the Breslov Research Institute
Explores the art of consciously observing Shabbat and understanding in-depth many of the day's spiritual practices. 5⅛ x 8¼, 224 pp, Deluxe PB w/flaps, ISBN 1-58023-175-6 **$18.95**

The Women's Passover Companion
Women's Reflections on the Festival of Freedom
Edited by Rabbi Sharon Cohen Anisfeld, Tara Mohr, and Catherine Spector
Groundbreaking. A provocative conversation about women's relationships to Passover as well as the roots and meanings of women's seders.
6 x 9, 352 pp, Hardcover, ISBN 1-58023-128-4 **$24.95**

The Women's Seder Sourcebook
Rituals & Readings for Use at the Passover Seder
Edited by Rabbi Sharon Cohen Anisfeld, Tara Mohr, and Catherine Spector
Gathers the voices of more than one hundred women in readings, personal and creative reflections, commentaries, blessings, and ritual suggestions that can be incorporated into your Passover celebration.
6 x 9, 384 pp, Hardcover, ISBN 1-58023-136-5 **$24.95**

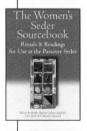

Creating Lively Passover Seders: A Sourcebook of Engaging Tales, Texts & Activities
By David Arnow, Ph.D. 7 x 9, 416 pp, Quality PB, ISBN 1-58023-184-5 **$24.99**

Hanukkah, 2nd Edition: The Family Guide to Spiritual Celebration
By Dr. Ron Wolfson. Edited by Joel Lurie Grishaver.
7 x 9, 240 pp, illus., Quality PB, ISBN 1-58023-122-5 **$18.95**

The Jewish Family Fun Book: Holiday Projects, Everyday Activities, and Travel Ideas with Jewish Themes *By Danielle Dardashti and Roni Sarig. Illus. by Avi Katz.*
6 x 9, 288 pp, 70+ b/w illus. & diagrams, Quality PB, ISBN 1-58023-171-3 **$18.95**

The Jewish Gardening Cookbook: Growing Plants & Cooking for
Holidays & Festivals *By Michael Brown* 6 x 9, 224 pp, 30+ illus., Quality PB, ISBN 1-58023-116-0 **$16.95**

The Jewish Lights Book of Fun Classroom Activities: Simple and Seasonal
Projects for Teachers and Students *By Danielle Dardashti and Roni Sarig*
6 x 9, 240 pp, Quality PB, ISBN 1–58023–206–X **$19.99**

Passover, 2nd Edition: The Family Guide to Spiritual Celebration
By Dr. Ron Wolfson with Joel Lurie Grishaver 7 x 9, 352 pp, Quality PB, ISBN 1-58023-174-8 **$19.95**

Shabbat, 2nd Edition: The Family Guide to Preparing for and Celebrating the Sabbath
By Dr. Ron Wolfson 7 x 9, 320 pp, illus., Quality PB, ISBN 1-58023-164-0 **$19.95**

Sharing Blessings: Children's Stories for Exploring the Spirit of the Jewish Holidays
By Rahel Musleah and Michael Klayman
8½ x 11, 64 pp, Full-color illus., Hardcover, ISBN 1-879045-71-0 **$18.95** *For ages 6 & up*

Life Cycle
Marriage / Parenting / Family / Aging

Jewish Fathers: A Legacy of Love
Photographs by Lloyd Wolf. Essays by Paula Wolfson. Foreword by Harold S. Kushner.
Honors the role of contemporary Jewish fathers in America. Each father tells in his own words what it means to be a parent and Jewish, and what he learned from his own father. Insightful photos. 9½ x 9⅜, 144 pp with 100+ duotone photos, Hardcover, ISBN 1-58023-204-3 **$30.00**

The New Jewish Baby Album: Creating and Celebrating the Beginning of a Spiritual Life—A Jewish Lights Companion
By the Editors at Jewish Lights. Foreword by Anita Diamant. Preface by Sandy Eisenberg Sasso.
A spiritual keepsake that will be treasured for generations. More than just a memory book, *shows you how—and why it's important*—to create a Jewish home and a Jewish life. 8 x 10, 64 pp, Deluxe Padded Hardcover, Full-color illus., ISBN 1-58023-138-1 **$19.95**

The Jewish Pregnancy Book: A Resource for the Soul, Body & Mind during Pregnancy, Birth & the First Three Months
By Sandy Falk, M.D., and Rabbi Daniel Judson, with Steven A. Rapp
Includes medical information, prayers and rituals for each stage of pregnancy, from a liberal Jewish perspective. 7 x 10, 208 pp, Quality PB, b/w illus., ISBN 1-58023-178-0 **$16.95**

Celebrating Your New Jewish Daughter: Creating Jewish Ways to Welcome Baby Girls into the Covenant—New and Traditional Ceremonies
By Debra Nussbaum Cohen 6 x 9, 272 pp, Quality PB, ISBN 1-58023-090-3 **$18.95**

The New Jewish Baby Book, 2nd Edition: Names, Ceremonies & Customs—A Guide for Today's Families *By Anita Diamant* 6 x 9, 336 pp, Quality PB, ISBN 1-58023-251-5 **$19.99**

Parenting As a Spiritual Journey: Deepening Ordinary and Extraordinary Events into Sacred Occasions *By Rabbi Nancy Fuchs-Kreimer* 6 x 9, 224 pp, Quality PB, ISBN 1-58023-016-4 **$16.95**

Judaism for Two: A Spiritual Guide for Strengthening and Celebrating Your Loving Relationship *By Rabbi Nancy Fuchs-Kreimer and Rabbi Nancy H. Wiener*
Addresses the ways Jewish teachings can enhance and strengthen committed relationships. 6 x 9, 208 pp, Quality PB, ISBN 1-58023-254-X **$16.99**

Embracing the Covenant: Converts to Judaism Talk About Why & How
By Rabbi Allan Berkowitz and Patti Moskovitz 6 x 9, 192 pp, Quality PB, ISBN 1-879045-50-8 **$16.95**

The Guide to Jewish Interfaith Family Life: An InterfaithFamily.com Handbook
Edited by Ronnie Friedland and Edmund Case 6 x 9, 384 pp, Quality PB, ISBN 1-58023-153-5 **$18.95**

Introducing My Faith and My Community
The Jewish Outreach Institute Guide for the Christian in a Jewish Interfaith Relationship
By Rabbi Kerry M. Olitzky 6 x 9, 176 pp, Quality PB, ISBN 1-58023-192-6 **$16.99**

Making a Successful Jewish Interfaith Marriage: The Jewish Outreach Institute Guide to Opportunities, Challenges and Resources
By Rabbi Kerry M. Olitzky with Joan Peterson Littman 6 x 9, 176 pp, Quality PB, ISBN 1-58023-170-5 **$16.95**

The Creative Jewish Wedding Book: A Hands-On Guide to New & Old Traditions, Ceremonies & Celebrations *By Gabrielle Kaplan-Mayer*
Provides the tools to create the most meaningful Jewish traditional or alternative wedding by using ritual elements to express your unique style and spirituality. 9 x 9, 288 pp, b/w photos, Quality PB, ISBN 1-58023-194-2 **$19.99**

Divorce Is a Mitzvah: A Practical Guide to Finding Wholeness and Holiness When Your Marriage Dies *By Rabbi Perry Netter. Afterword by Rabbi Laura Geller.*
6 x 9, 224 pp, Quality PB, ISBN 1-58023-172-1 **$16.95**

A Heart of Wisdom: Making the Jewish Journey from Midlife through the Elder Years
Edited by Susan Berrin. Foreword by Harold Kushner. 6 x 9, 384 pp, Quality PB, ISBN 1-58023-051-2 **$18.95**

So That Your Values Live On: Ethical Wills and How to Prepare Them
Edited by Jack Riemer and Nathaniel Stampfer 6 x 9, 272 pp, Quality PB, ISBN 1-879045-34-6 **$18.95**

Spirituality/Women's Interest

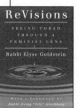

The Quotable Jewish Woman: Wisdom, Inspiration & Humor from the Mind & Heart *Edited and compiled by Elaine Bernstein Partnow*
The definitive collection of ideas, reflections, humor, and wit of over 300 Jewish women.
6 x 9, 496 pp, Hardcover, ISBN 1-58023-193-4 **$29.99**

Lifecycles, Vol. 1: Jewish Women on Life Passages & Personal Milestones
Edited and with introductions by Rabbi Debra Orenstein 6 x 9, 480 pp, Quality PB, ISBN 1-58023-018-0 **$19.95**

Lifecycles, Vol. 2: Jewish Women on Biblical Themes in Contemporary Life
Edited and with introductions by Rabbi Debra Orenstein and Rabbi Jane Rachel Litman
6 x 9, 464 pp, Quality PB, ISBN 1-58023-019-9 **$19.95**

Moonbeams: A Hadassah Rosh Hodesh Guide *Edited by Carol Diament, Ph.D.*
8½ x 11, 240 pp, Quality PB, ISBN 1-58023-099-7 **$20.00**

ReVisions: Seeing Torah through a Feminist Lens *By Rabbi Elyse Goldstein*
5½ x 8½, 224 pp, Quality PB, ISBN 1-58023-117-9 **$16.95**

White Fire: A Portrait of Women Spiritual Leaders in America
By Rabbi Malka Drucker. Photographs by Gay Block.
7 x 10, 320 pp, 30+ b/w photos, Hardcover, ISBN 1-893361-64-0 **$24.95** *(A SkyLight Paths book)*

Women of the Wall: Claiming Sacred Ground at Judaism's Holy Site
Edited by Phyllis Chesler and Rivka Haut 6 x 9, 496 pp, b/w photos, Hardcover, ISBN 1-58023-161-6 **$34.95**

The Women's Haftarah Commentary: New Insights from Women Rabbis on the 54 Weekly Haftarah Portions, the 5 Megillot & Special Shabbatot
Edited by Rabbi Elyse Goldstein 6 x 9, 560 pp, Hardcover, ISBN 1-58023-133-0 **$39.99**

The Women's Torah Commentary: New Insights from Women Rabbis on the 54 Weekly Torah Portions *Edited by Rabbi Elyse Goldstein*
6 x 9, 496 pp, Hardcover, ISBN 1-58023-076-8 **$34.95**

The Year Mom Got Religion: One Woman's Midlife Journey into Judaism
By Lee Meyerhoff Hendler 6 x 9, 208 pp, Quality PB, ISBN 1-58023-070-9 **$15.95**

See Holidays for *The Women's Passover Companion: Women's Reflections on the Festival of Freedom* and *The Women's Seder Sourcebook: Rituals & Readings for Use at the Passover Seder.* Also see Bar/Bat Mitzvah for *The JGirl's Guide: The Young Jewish Woman's Handbook for Coming of Age.*

Travel

Israel—A Spiritual Travel Guide, 2nd Edition
A Companion for the Modern Jewish Pilgrim
By Rabbi Lawrence A. Hoffman 4¼ x 10, 256 pp, Quality PB, illus., ISBN 1-58023-261-2 **$18.99**
Also Available: **The Israel Mission Leader's Guide** ISBN 1-58023-085-7 **$4.95**

12 Steps

100 Blessings Every Day Daily Twelve Step Recovery Affirmations, Exercises for Personal Growth & Renewal Reflecting Seasons of the Jewish Year
By Rabbi Kerry M. Olitzky. Foreword by Rabbi Neil Gillman.
One-day-at-a-time monthly format. Reflects on the rhythm of the Jewish calendar to bring insight to recovery from addictions.
4½ x 6½, 432 pp, Quality PB, ISBN 1-879045-30-3 **$15.99**

Recovery from Codependence: A Jewish Twelve Steps Guide to Healing Your Soul
By Rabbi Kerry M. Olitzky 6 x 9, 160 pp, Quality PB, ISBN 1-879045-32-X **$13.95**

Renewed Each Day: Daily Twelve Step Recovery Meditations Based on the Bible
By Rabbi Kerry M. Olitzky and Aaron Z.
Vol. 1—Genesis & Exodus: 6 x 9, 224 pp, Quality PB, ISBN 1-879045-12-5 **$14.95**
Vol. 2—Leviticus, Numbers & Deuteronomy: 6 x 9, 280 pp, Quality PB, ISBN 1-879045-13-3 **$14.95**

Twelve Jewish Steps to Recovery: A Personal Guide to Turning from Alcoholism & Other Addictions—Drugs, Food, Gambling, Sex...
By Rabbi Kerry M. Olitzky and Stuart A. Copans, M.D. Preface by Abraham J. Twerski, M.D.
6 x 9, 144 pp, Quality PB, ISBN 1-879045-09-5 **$14.95**

Bar/Bat Mitzvah

I Am Jewish
Personal Reflections Inspired by the Last Words of Daniel Pearl

Almost 150 Jews—both famous and not—from all walks of life, from all around the world, write about Identity, Heritage, Covenant / Chosenness and Faith, Humanity and Ethnicity, and *Tikkun Olam* and Justice.

Edited by Judea and Ruth Pearl
6 x 9, 304 pp, Deluxe PB w/flaps, ISBN 1-58023-259-0 **$18.99**; Hardcover, ISBN 1-58023-183-7 **$24.99**
**Download a free copy of the *I Am Jewish Teacher's Guide* at our website:
www.jewishlights.com**

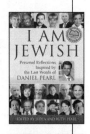

The JGirl's Guide: The Young Jewish Woman's Handbook for Coming of Age
By Penina Adelman, Ali Feldman, and Shulamit Reinharz
An inspirational, interactive guidebook designed to help pre-teen Jewish girls address the spiritual, educational, and psychological issues surrounding coming of age in today's society. 6 x 9, 224 pp, Quality PB, ISBN 1-58023-215-9 **$14.99**
Also Available: **The JGirl's Teacher's and Parent's Guide**
8½ x 11, 56 pp, PB, ISBN 1-58023-225-6 **$8.99**

Bar/Bat Mitzvah Basics: A Practical Family Guide to Coming of Age Together
By Helen Leneman 6 x 9, 240 pp, Quality PB, ISBN 1-58023-151-9 **$18.95**

The Bar/Bat Mitzvah Memory Book: An Album for Treasuring the Spiritual Celebration
By Rabbi Jeffrey K. Salkin and Nina Salkin
8 x 10, 48 pp, Deluxe Hardcover, 2-color text, ribbon marker, ISBN 1-58023-111-X **$19.95**

For Kids—Putting God on Your Guest List: How to Claim the Spiritual Meaning of Your Bar or Bat Mitzvah *By Rabbi Jeffrey K. Salkin*
6 x 9, 144 pp, Quality PB, ISBN 1-58023-015-6 **$14.99** *For ages 11–12*

Putting God on the Guest List, 3rd Edition: How to Reclaim the Spiritual Meaning of Your Child's Bar or Bat Mitzvah *By Rabbi Jeffrey K. Salkin*
6 x 9, 224 pp, Quality PB, ISBN 1-58023-222-1 **$16.99**; Hardcover, ISBN 1-58023-260-4 **$24.99**

Tough Questions Jews Ask: A Young Adult's Guide to Building a Jewish Life
By Rabbi Edward Feinstein 6 x 9, 160 pp, Quality PB, ISBN 1-58023-139-X **$14.99** *For ages 13 & up*
Also Available: **Tough Questions Jews Ask Teacher's Guide**
8½ x 11, 72 pp, PB, ISBN 1-58023-187-X **$8.95**

Bible Study/Midrash

Hineini in Our Lives: Learning How to Respond to Others through 14 Biblical Texts, and Personal Stories *By Norman J. Cohen* 6 x 9, 240 pp, Hardcover, ISBN 1-58023-131-4 **$23.95**

Ancient Secrets: Using the Stories of the Bible to Improve Our Everyday Lives
By Rabbi Levi Meier, Ph.D. 5½ x 8½, 288 pp, Quality PB, ISBN 1-58023-064-4 **$16.95**

Moses—The Prince, the Prophet: His Life, Legend & Message for Our Lives
By Rabbi Levi Meier, Ph.D. 6 x 9, 224 pp, Quality PB, ISBN 1-58023-069-5 **$16.95**

Self, Struggle & Change: Family Conflict Stories in Genesis and Their Healing Insights for Our Lives *By Norman J. Cohen* 6 x 9, 224 pp, Quality PB, ISBN 1-879045-66-4 **$18.99**

Voices from Genesis: Guiding Us through the Stages of Life *By Norman J. Cohen*
6 x 9, 192 pp, Quality PB, ISBN 1-58023-118-7 **$16.95**

Congregation Resources

Becoming a Congregation of Learners: Learning as a Key to Revitalizing Congregational Life *By Isa Aron, Ph.D. Foreword by Rabbi Lawrence A. Hoffman.*
6 x 9, 304 pp, Quality PB, ISBN 1-58023-089-X **$19.95**

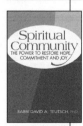

Spiritual Community: The Power to Restore Hope, Commitment and Joy
By Rabbi David A. Teutsch, PhD
5½ x 8½, 144 pp, Hardcover, ISBN 1-58023-270-1 **$19.99**

Jewish Pastoral Care, 2nd Edition: A Practical Handbook from Traditional & Contemporary Sources *Edited by Rabbi Dayle A. Friedman*
6 x 9, 464 pp, Hardcover, ISBN 1-58023-221-3 **$40.00**

The Self-Renewing Congregation: Organizational Strategies for Revitalizing Congregational Life *By Isa Aron, Ph.D. Foreword by Dr. Ron Wolfson.*
6 x 9, 304 pp, Quality PB, ISBN 1-58023-166-7 **$19.95**

About Jewish Lights

People of all faiths and backgrounds yearn for books that attract, engage, educate, and spiritually inspire.

Our principal goal is to stimulate thought and help all people learn about who the Jewish People are, where they come from, and what the future can be made to hold. While people of our diverse Jewish heritage are the primary audience, our books speak to people in the Christian world as well and will broaden their understanding of Judaism and the roots of their own faith.

We bring to you authors who are at the forefront of spiritual thought and experience. While each has something different to say, they all say it in a voice that you can hear.

Our books are designed to welcome you and then to engage, stimulate, and inspire. We judge our success not only by whether or not our books are beautiful and commercially successful, but by whether or not they make a difference in your life.

For your information and convenience, at the back of this book we have provided a list of other Jewish Lights books you might find interesting and useful. They cover all the categories of your life:

Bar/Bat Mitzvah	Life Cycle
Bible Study / Midrash	Meditation
Children's Books	Parenting
Congregation Resources	Prayer
Current Events / History	Ritual / Sacred Practice
Ecology	Spirituality
Fiction: Mystery, Science Fiction	Theology / Philosophy
Grief / Healing	Travel
Holidays / Holy Days	Twelve Steps
Inspiration	Women's Interest
Kabbalah / Mysticism / Enneagram	

Stuart M. Matlins

Stuart M. Matlins, Publisher

Or phone, fax, mail or e-mail to: **JEWISH LIGHTS Publishing**
Sunset Farm Offices, Route 4 • P.O. Box 237 • Woodstock, Vermont 05091
Tel: (802) 457-4000 • Fax: (802) 457-4004 • www.jewishlights.com
Credit card orders: (800) 962-4544 (8:30AM–5:30PM ET Monday–Friday)
Generous discounts on quantity orders. SATISFACTION GUARANTEED. Prices subject to change.